THE PROCEEDINGS
of the
6th INTERNATIONAL HUMANITIES CONFERENCE

All & Everything 2001

THE PROCEEDINGS

THE PROCEEDINGS OF THE 6th INTERNATIONAL HUMANITIES CONFERENCE

ALL & EVERYTHING 2001

Anthony Blake
Keith Buzzell
Wim van Dullemen
Ana Fragomeni
Seymour Ginsburg
John Perrott
Bert Sharp
Nicholas Tereshchenko
Professor M. W. Thring

Published by All & Everything Conferences
2010

Second Edition Published 2010
Published by All & Everything Conferences (on behalf of the Planning Committee)
© Copyright 2010 by Seymour B. Ginsburg and Ian C. MacFarlane

First Edition Privately Published 2001
Published by the Conveners of the International Humanities Conference: All and Everything 2001
© 2001 Seymour B. Ginsburg, Dr. H. J. Sharp, and Marlena O'Hagan-Buzzell

The contents of this publication may not be reproduced or copied in whole or part in any book, magazine, periodical, pamphlet, circular, information storage or data retrieval system, or in any other form without the written permission of the Planning Committee.

Any profit from the sale of these Proceedings will be devoted to the funds for the organization of future Conferences of a similar nature.

Published by All & Everything Conferences

Website: www.aandeconference.org
Email: info@aandeconference.org

Second Edition eBook

ISBN-10: 1-905578-21-0
ISBN-13: 978-1-905578-21-4

Also Published as
Second Edition Print

ISBN-10: 1-905578-20-2
ISBN-13: 978-1-905578-20-7

Table of Contents

Foreword 5
Conference Program 7
Advisory Board 10
Speakers 12
In Memorium - Michael Smyth 15
In Memorium - Joyce Sharp 16
Gurdjieff's Legominisms in Paris - Salle Pleyel 17
The Psychology of Transformation 25
Beelzebub Restores our Understanding of Teleology and Ontology 31
Beelzebub Restores our Understanding of Teleology and Ontology - Questions & Answers 40
Seminar 1 - Chapters 3, 4 & 5 of Beelzebub's Tales to His Grandson 45
Seminar 2 - Chapters 3, 4 & 5 of Beelzebub's Tales to His Grandson (continued) 50
Informal Recollections of Meetings with Gurdjieff and Ouspensky 62
To Destroy Mercilessly… 75
To Destroy Mercilessly… - Questions & Answers 79
Seminar 3 - Chapter 6 & 7 of Beelzebub's Tales 87
Duversity 97
Higher Being Bodies: Their Origins and Functioning 104
On Higher Being-Bodies: The Gurdjieffian View 112
Higher Being Bodies: The Gurdjieffian View - Questions & Answers 117
Seminar 5 - Oskiano 124
Where Do We Go From Here? 132
Appendix 1 - Review of Beelzebub's Tales to His Grandson in Russian 144
Appendix 2 - List of Attendees 156
Index 157

Foreword

The International Humanities Conference - All & Everything returned to Bognor Regis, England and for the year 2001. Once again, the conferees came from a number of different countries, preserving the international character of the event. Many of the attendees from past years who were unable to travel to the States returned to Bognor, and many friends from the conference in the States joined us in England. In addition, several people were first time attendees.

The presentations this year offered a broad experience. The program included presentations on aspects of *Beelzebub's Tales*, a performance of Gurdjieff/de Hartmann music, a narrated Movements demonstration, a presentation on sacred geometry and Professor Thring's recollections of his meetings with Gurdjieff and Ouspensky. The afternoon discussions focused on chapters 3 through 7 of *Beelzebub's Tales to His Grandson* and the general theme of Oskiano.

Once again, the topic of "to tape or not to tape..." was considered by the conferees. A consensus was reached to tape record the Q&A's and the seminars. The manner of recording, however, resulted in less than excellent quality tapes leaving our presenters and facilitators with the arduous task of transcribing nearly inaudible tapes. Back to the drawing board with the technical support team!

The reader will note that there is no written record of the Movements Presentation given by Wim. Van Dulleman and performed by Christiane Macketanz. The video tape of Movements was not shown since it was intended as a backup for the live Movements presentation.

*   *   *

The Planning Committee wishes to thank Professor Holly Baggett, Dr. Leon Schlamm and Professor Karen-Claire Voss for their support in serving on the Advisory Board. We wish to welcome Professor Wallace Martin and Professor Jon Woodson to the Advisory Board.

*   *   *

The Individual Presenters were responsible for providing a written paper and /or a computer disc covering the material they have presented at the conference and also for the transcription of their particular question and answer session at the end of their presentation.

The responsibility of the compilation and editing for a final draft suitable for printing has largely been the responsibility of Marlena Buzzell. Please accept her apology for any typographical errors, omissions or contextual errors.

Conference Program

THE INTERNATIONAL HUMANITIES CONFERENCE

All & Everything

2001

A Gathering of the Companions of the Book

March 28 April 1, 2001

The Royal Norfolk Hotel
Bognor Regis
England

<u>*Organizing Committee*</u>
USA
Seymour B. Ginsburg, Patricia Bennett, Marlena Buzzell
Europe
Frank Brzeski, H.J. Sharp, John Scullion

All & Everything Conference 2001

CONFERENCE PROGRAM

Day 1 Wednesday March 28
15.00-17.00 Meeting of the Planning Committee

20.00-21.15 Getting to know you session.
Informal.

Delegates to be welcomed by Marlena Buzzell on behalf of the Planning Committee.

Session 1

21.15-22.00 **Legominisms in Paris**
Ana Fragomeni

Day 2 Thursday March 29
08.00-09.00 Sitting

09.00-09.45 Introduction. Pat Bennett.
Greetings, messages, announcements, Copying, recording and ordering Facilities. List of addresses for future Contact and exchanges.

History and genesis of the conference By Bert Sharp.

Session 2
09.45-11.00 **The Three Story Diagram**
John Perrott
11.00-11.30 Morning coffee

Session 3
11.30-12.45 **Gurdjieff Restores Teleology and Ontology**
Prof. M. Thring

12.45-14.30 Lunch Break

Seminar 1
14.30-15.30 Chapters 3,4&5 of **Beelzebub's Tales to His Grandson**
Facilitator: Sophia Wellbeloved

15.30-16.00 Afternoon Tea

Seminar 2
16.00-17.00 Continuation of Seminar 1
Facilitator: Bonnie Phillips

Day 3 Friday March 30
08.00-09.00 Sitting

Session 5
09.30-10.45 **To Destroy Mercilessly**
Keith Buzzell
10.45-11.15 Morning coffee

Session 6
11.15-12.30 **A Taste of the Sacred**. A Description of some of the Operating principles of Gurdjieff's Movements
Wim Van Dulleman

12.30-14.30 Lunch Break

Seminar 3

14.30-15.30 Chapters 6 and 7 of
Beelzebub's Tales to His Grandson
Facilitator: Tony Blake

15.30-16.00 Afternoon Tea

16.00-17.00 Continuation of Seminar 3
Facilitator: Tony Blake

Conference Programme

Session 7
20.00-21.00 **Gurdjieff Movements Video**
    Wim van Dulleman

Session 8
21.00-22.00 **Duversity**
    Tony Blake

Day 4 Saturday March 31
08.00-09.00 Sitting

Session 9
09.30-10.45 **Higher Being Bodies: Their Origin and Functioning**
    H.J. Sharp

Session 9   [continuation]
    On Higher Being Bodies, the Gurdjieffian View
    Sy Ginsburg and Nicholas Tereshchenko

10.45-11.15 Morning coffee

Session 10
11.15-12.30 Continuing discussion of mornings Presentation

12.30-14.30 Lunch

Seminar 5
14.30-15.30 **Oskiano**
    Facilitator: Nick Bryce

15.30-16.00 Afternoon Tea

Seminar 6
16.00-17.00 **Oskiano**
    Facilitator: Nick Bryce

19.30-21.30 **Piano Recitals**
    Wim van Dulleman

Day 5 Sunday April 1
08:00-09:00 Sitting

Session 11
09:30-10:00 **Open Forum:
Where do we go from here?**
Facilitator: Sy Ginsburg

10.30-11.00 Morning coffee

Session 12
11.00-12.00 **Open Forum**
    Continuation of previous session
Conference Ends.

Advisory Board

PROFESSOR MASASHI ASAI holds the chair of English Literature and Cultural Studies at Kyoto Tachibana Women's University and has made a significant contribution to studies of D.H. Lawrence (who visited the Prieure in February 1924]. As an undergraduate in Kyoto, he contacted a working group [which he now leads] instituted by Gurdjieffians from California. His unprecedented contributions to the dissemination of Gurdjieff's ideas in Japan include the translation *of Beelzebub's Tales to His Grandson, Life is Real Only Then, When "I am", In Search of the Miraculous* and James Moore's, *Gurdjieff, The Anatomy of a Myth*.

J. WALTER DRISCOLL is an independent scholar focused on Gurdjieff studies since the 1960's. He met and corresponded with Wilhelm Nyland and his groups in Warwick, NJ and Seattle from 1970 until Nyland's death in 1975. Following postgraduate training in 1978, he embarked on his major work *Gurdjieff an Annotated Bibliography* [Garland Publishing, 1985] in collaboration with The Gurdjieff Foundation of California. He is now engaged on a second edition for which he solicits material and is associate editor of the "Gurdjieff Homepage" at www.gurdjieff.org. He assisted George Baker with *Gurdjieff in America: An Overview* [American Alternative Religions, 1995].

WIM VAN DULLEMEN is a Dutch musician and musicologist who have placed his gifts at the service of the Work. Shortly after completing his studies under the composer W. Wijdeveld and becoming a professional concert pianist he had a crucial meeting [in 1968] with J. G. Bennett. For 13 years he was the Class pianist for the eminent French Movements teacher Solange Claustres. He has propagated the Gurdjieff/de Hartmann musical 'oeuvre' in 'workshops', articles, courses, lectures, and concerts - sometimes independently and sometimes in collaboration with Mme Claustres and the French pianist Alain Kremski.

DR. MASSIMO INTROVIGNE is managing director of CESNUR, the Centre for Studies on New Religions in Torino, Italy. CESNUR's library hosts one of the most significant collections of Fourth Way Books in Southern Europe. He teaches at Queen of The Apostles University in Rome and is the author of twenty books in the field of sociology of religion and contemporary esotericism. He has lectured often and sympathetically on Fourth Way-related subjects.

PROFESSOR WALLACE MARTIN teaches modern literature and critical theory at the University of Toledo. His writings include '*The New Age' Under Orage*.

DR. H J. SHARP took a first degree is Physiology and an M. Sc. in Metallurgy by private study while working in industry. He later earned his Ph.D. in Material Science. Subsequently, he has become involved in psychological transformation of himself and others, a much more difficult endeavour. In this he has been helped by many including Ronald and Murial Oldham and Lewis

Advisory Board

Creed, when he was able to visit the Dicker, John Castanios Flores, who led a large Work group in Mexico and came to Littlehampton to end his days, and by Nicholas Tereshchenko and Sy Ginsburg. There have been many others speaking through the written page and in other ways and perhaps most of all, in a special way, his dear wife and daughter.

PROFESSOR PAUL BEEKMAN TAYLOR [who for the past 30 years held the chair of Medieval English languages and literature at the University of Geneva] grew up at the Prieure and was thus from earliest childhood immersed in a Gurdjieffian milieu. Later adopted by Jean Toomer, he lived in New York City and Doylestown, Pennsylvania, and after the war sustained contact with Gurdjieff in New York and Paris. He has published ten books and over a hundred articles. Published in 1998, *Shadows of Heaven: Toomer and Gurdjieff* [Samuel Weiser, Inc.] draws on his and his mother's experiences with both men. His most recent book *is Gurdjieff and Orage: Brothers in Elysium.* [Samuel Weiser, Inc. 2001].

PROFESSOR JON WOODSON is a Professor of English on the faculty of Howard University in Washington, D.C. He is the author of *To Make a New Race: Gurdjieff, Toomer, and the Harlem Renaissance* [University of Mississippi Press, 1999]. Since commencing work on his doctoral dissertation on the poet Melvin B. Tolson in 1973, he has researched and published in the area of Fourth Way concepts as they have been employed in modern literature.

Speakers

Keith A. Buzzell, D.O.

Dr. Buzzell is a 1960 graduate of the Philadelphia College of Osteopathic Medicine. He met Irmis Popoff [N.Y. Foundation] in 1971 and formed groups under her supervision into the 1980s. Buzzell met Annie Lou Staveley, founder of the Two Rivers Farm in Oregon, in 1988 and maintained a Work relationship with her up to her death. He continues group Work in Bridgton, ME.

Seymour B. [Sy] Ginsburg, J.D.

Sy Ginsburg was born in Chicago in 1934 and currently resides in Florida. He was introduced to the Gurdjieff Work by Sri Madhava Ashish, an eminent theosophical scholar and Hindu monk, who became his mentor over a 19 year period. Ginsburg was a member of the Gurdjieff Society of Florida and later a co-founder of the Gurdjieff Institute of Florida. Currently, he is a Director of The Theosophical Society in Miami & South Florida and facilitator of the Gurdjieff Study Group at The Theosophical Society.

H. J. Sharp, Ph.D.

Dr. Sharp took a first degree in Physiology and a M.Sc. in Metallurgy by private study while working in industry. He later earned his PhD. in Material Science. Subsequently he has become involved in psychological transformation of himself and others, a much more difficult endeavour. In this he has been helped by many, including Ronald and Murial Oldham and Lewis Creed, when he was able to visit the Dicker, John Castanios Flores, who led a large Work group in Mexico and came to Littlehampton to end his days, and Nicolas Tereshchenko and Sy Ginsburg. There have been many others speaking through the written page and in other ways and perhaps most of all, in a special way, his dear wife and daughter.

Wim van Dullemen

Win is a Dutch musician and musicologist who have placed his gifts at the service of the Work. Shortly after completing his studies under the composer W. Wijdeveki and becoming a professional concert pianist, he had a crucial meeting [in 1968] with J. G. Bennett. For 13 years he was the Class pianist for the eminent French Movements teacher Solange Claustres. He has propagated the Gurdjieff/de Hartmann musical "oeuvre" in 'workshops', articles, courses, lectures, and concerts - sometimes independently and sometimes in collaboration with Mme Claustres and the French pianist Akin Kremski.

Speakers

Ana Fragomeni

Graduating with a degree in architecture in 1962 from ANF - The University of Brazil, Rio de Janeiro, Ana pursued post-graduate studies in Computer Science. She worked as Planning and Organizing Coordinator for the finance ministry and further developed her administrative skills at IAAP Paris in 1978.

Since her youth she has been continuously interested in 'all and everything', exploring several paths of self development, esoteric studies and symbology until, in 1982, the books of Mouravieff and Ouspensky led her to the Fourth Way. She joined Durval Teixeira's group [Uberlandia, MG] and participated in the Work which was led in Brazil under the general direction of Natalie de Salzmann.

In 1990 she retired from public service and, with three children grown, she devoted herself to the study and propagation of Gurdjieff's teaching. She opened as small publishing house [Editora Gilgamesh] and maintained the web-site 4C-Gurdjieff Brazil at www.4C.com.br. Having been introduced to the A&E Conferences by Nicholas Tereshchenko, Ana attended the 2000 conference, giving an informal presentation on the enneagrammatic structure on the life and writings of Gurdjieff.

She is the author of the *Dicionario Enciclopedico de Informatica* [Infomatics Encyclopaedic Dictionary - English and Portugese], published in 1986 by Ed. Campus, Sao Paulo.

In addition to her primary interest which encompasses Work and the Enneagram, she has now embarked upon a historical and cultural research and study of art, music and sacred architecture.

John Perrott

John's introduction to 'the Work' was in 1964 as a visitor to a 'Work Sunday" at Coomb Springs, Kingston. J G Bennett was the director of studies and it was a time of conflict between the old guard Gurdjieff System adherents, the Subud Lobby, and those like John who embraced both.

While pursuing his career with IBM [UK] Ltd., John attended anything he was permitted. Later John pursued Sufi Studies, still under J.G.B. while working as a systems director in Yeovil; he also led Work groups in Somerset. After a decade of ex-patriot Consultancy in the M.E., SE Asia and Europe, he worked under "Chief" a.k.a. Gary Chicoine until the late '80's.

He then languished for years, convinced that it all had come to nothing, until the intervention of the first All & Everything Conference, which has transformed his life and that of his wife, Alison. This introduced him to Russell Smith. As a result he now clearly perceives that the missing factor was the general inattention to Gurdjieff's "Third Obligolnian Striving", the quintessence of the 4th Way.

He now shares his time between the 'Dog', Texas and England, helping in 4th Way teaching, particularly in the context of the Third Striving. He takes students at no charge on a one to one basis and conducts a weekly group to assist those studying *'Cosmic Secrets'*.

Professor M. W. Thring, ScD. FEng.

M. W. Thring was professor of Mechanical Engineering, Queen Mary College, London University, from 1963 to 1981. Besides many academic publications Professor Thring has published many books including *Man, Machines and Tomorrow* [1973], *Machines-Masters or Slaves of Man* [1973, Ed with R.J. Crookes]; *Energy and Humanity* [1974]; *How to Invent* [1977 with E.R Lathwaite]; *The Engineer's Conscience* [1980]; and Robots and Telechirs [1983].

Professor Thring has been a student of G. I. Gurdjieff's ideas since 1937 when he attended lectures given by P. D. Ouspensky in London. He also studied with G .I. Gurdjieff in Paris in 1948.

In Memorium - Michael Smyth

Michael Smyth
1949-2001

"...nevertheless it does sometimes happen there that certain of them by chance escape this common fate and that instead of that automatic-Reason which has become usual there, a genuine objective 'being-Reason' is formed in certain of them as it is in all three-centered beings of our great Megalocosmos."

In Memorium - Joyce Sharp

In memory of H. J. Sharp's beloved wife Joyce Sharp who died December 31, 2000. Marjorie Joyce Wilson was born June 3 1920 in Bedford, Middlesex. She and Bert were married April 26, 1943. Their daughter, Christine Silvia Iris Sharp was born May 14, 1944.

The spirit which does not wear
the garment of Love
should never have been.
Its being is just shame.

Be drunken with Love,
for Love is all that exists.
Where is intimacy found,
if not in the give and take of Love?

If they ask what is Love,
say, the sacrifice of will.
If you have not left will behind,
you have no will at all.

The Lover is a king of kings
with both worlds beneath him;
and a king does not regard
what lies at his feet.

Jelaluddin Rumi

Gurdjieff's Legominisms in Paris - Salle Pleyel

Ana Helena Fragomeni

I will talk about something not very well known, that maybe it is not quite true, and it is also possible that it is not new for you. However, it was new for me and also very interesting. I bring this subject here because, if it is true, something very precious can be threatened - and many Legominisms more can exist thereabout, waiting to be interpreted and also in risk of transformation or destruction.

Two years ago, being very interested in the Enneagram, I was seeking that symbol and their meanings everywhere I went, in whatever I have read, and in all events and experiences I passed through. Nevertheless, I was totally unprepared for the meeting with the Legominisms I have found in Paris.

Entering a building open to the public, I came across a perfect circle in the floor, in white marble. There were also three marks in black marble at the borders of this circle, like arrows pointing to the centre. A certain angular irregularity in the places of these arrows draw my attention, together with another irregularity in the central corridor's line, which had a slight inclination in relation to the main entrance, with an angle not easily justifiable from the architectural point of view. I immediately associated the circle and the three arrows to the Enneagram, noticing that the arrows fitted exactly the circle division in nine parts. Besides, the arrows indicated three directions to follow starting from the centre of the circle, so indicating the three fundamental parts of the building.

I was very excited, mostly for knowing that Gurdjieff had been there, so this was probably a Fourth Way's people work. Very glad with this simple discovery, I went on visiting the interior of the building. I was sure that the Enneagram there in the floor was something done after Gurdjieff's death.

The building, although not too recent, has an interesting and nice architectural simplicity; cosy and elegant, with sober spaces that nowadays we would call a "clean" style. Some details in iron of the interior garnishment were impressing due to a quite significant geometric design. I had before me a collection of triangles laying on a special pattern; most of them with about ten golden little balls in its interior, as the Pythagorean tetrakys.

Suddenly, I began to feel like Alice in Wonderland, although figuring those interpretations were only a fruit of my deep immersion in the master's system. There it was the Ray of Creation, as a frame for the elevator, formed by a column of seven triangles. Each triangle, in its turn, was formed by three descending triangles full of gilded balls, and an empty ascending triangle at the middle. It was clearly an octave as well as three octaves in one. In the balustrade of the stairway, there were alternated again in each stage seven triangles. And more, at the top of a high pilaster I could see a capital with three glided triangles, also in a column pattern.

There was really something magic in the air. I didn't want to leave the building. I returned to the entrance, noticing the internal columns, which seemed thick tees in an immense forest. However, the columns didn't seem to obey a logical and immediately visible structural design. There was not a correct alignment linking the central corridor's columns - which formed two lateral corridors, as in a church aisle - to the columns of the hall - that surrounded the circle like trees around a glade.

Gurdjieff's Legominisms in Paris - Salle Pleyel

Now was the moment to analyze the structure of reinforced concrete, which seemed to have much more columns than needed to support that simple and modest building and their shafts were too thick. But the columns around of the circle - they were in number of nine!
Well, that gave me a shock! The Enneagram could not have been placed there later, because it was an integral part of the structural design! So, who was to attribute the project now? If Gurdjieff used the building at certain period, obviously it was built before that period.

I tried to obtain information about the construction and the architectural design. It was very difficult. I have studied the plans of the building, which I sketched during my visits to the place and corrected them later with the help of some photos I took there, and extra information. The building had been sold to private owners, and there was a petition made by a Senator to the Minister of Education, asking for some measures to be taken by the French government or by the Mayor of Paris, due to the building's great information for my interest. Some of it mentioned its splendid acoustical implementation.

One night, buying a ticket, I attended there a musical event. As I had already worked with this, I could really appreciate the remarkable acoustical design. The following year, returning there, I found the central colonnade enclosed by red silk strings to hinder the access.

Finally, I reached to the following conclusions:

1st - The plan of the ground floor shows a clear analogy with the plans of the chief Gothic Cathedrals, not only in the overall proportions, the atrium and the location of the labyrinth (the Enneagram), but specially in the central nave and the two lateral aisles. In addition, the sun orientation of the building also coincides with that of the great cathedrals.

2nd - The angular break in the line that goes from the entrance through the nave, which usually would be a straight line, turns to be the most interesting feature, not only for being the detail that draws attention to the intentionality of the design, but because it presents the same shift in the axis of the Egyptian Temples of Amon in Luxor, and that of Isis, P1hiiae Island on the Nile.

3rd - Analyzing the plan of the ground pavement we can notice the use of the golden section, chief characteristic of objective art, a clue of something that was properly made, with intention, by qualified people.

4th - The nine columns around the white marble circle could characterize a simple regular enneagon, and that would already be something quite rare in architecture. However, the three black arrows are strategically positioned, guiding the internal circulation in the building. Although they point to the centre and not to the exterior of the circle, they attribute special meaning to the three parts of the construction, a fact that gives them a great importance. This we can interpreted by the Enneagram, because they correspond, surely, to the number 4 at the entrance, to the number 2 where one of them points to the section of studies and to the number 9 where another one points to the chief functional part of the complex.

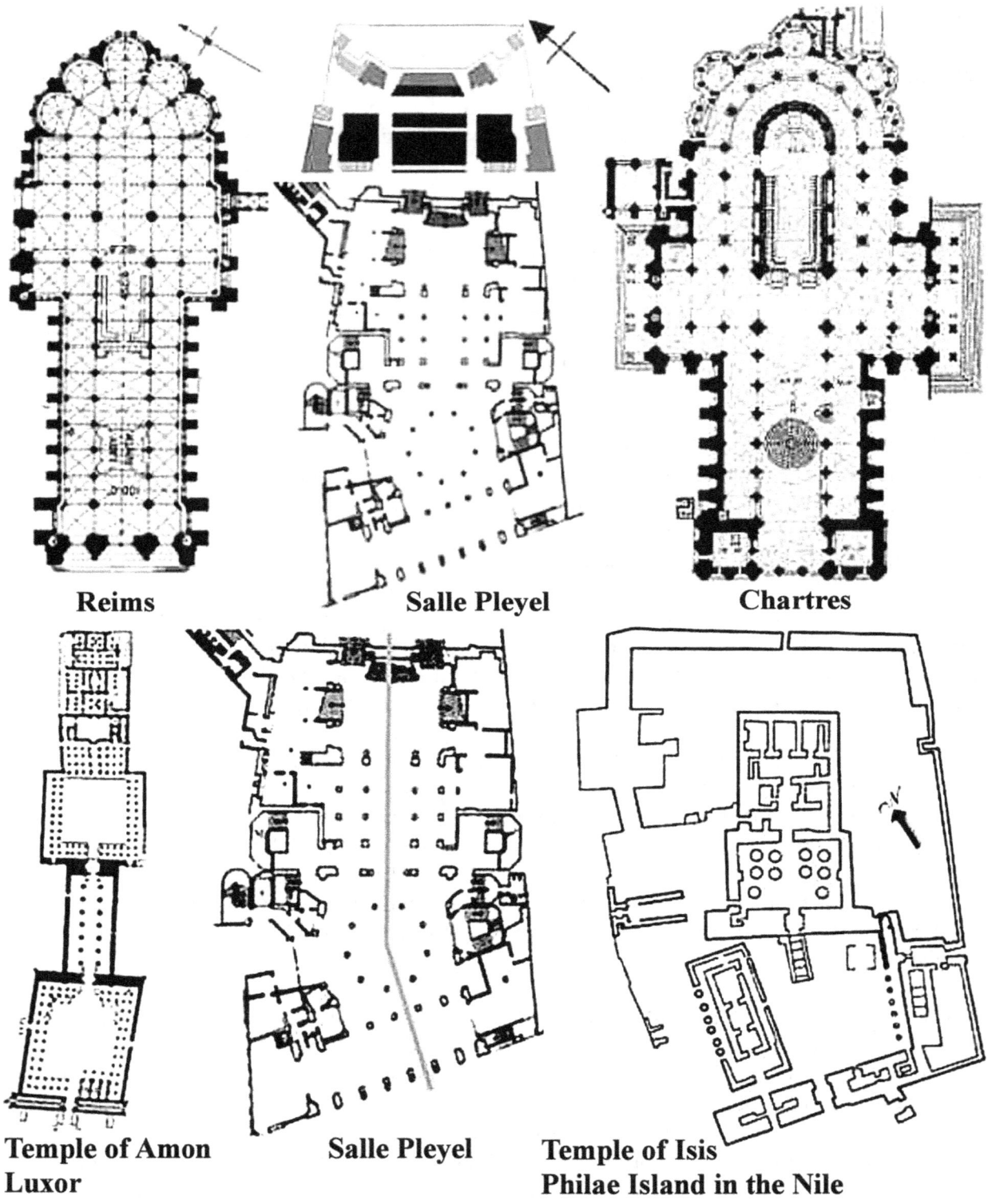

5th - The vestibule, or entrance hall, has the floor in colure marble, with exceedingly beautiful geometric patterns of triangles and unusual hexagons. This floor looks like that of Amiens Cathedral.

Festspielhaus Hellerau

6th - The front, perfectly integrated in the architecture that surrounds it, it is not easily noticed, because there is no point of view from which to discern the total perspective. The front is clear and limpid as a Doric Greek temple – or the colonnaded Hellerau. Horizontally divide in nine panels of windows, it has seven floors in nine panels of windows, it has seven floors in the street front, marked as if they were three, with another one, at the top, like a frieze with nine round windows or oculus. The module 9 is not common architecture, it is only found in few cases, as the Doric Temple of Hera ("Basilica"), in Paestum, near Naples, the Basilica of Euphrasius (worship, prayer and concert's place), in Porec, Croatia, and some medieval defensive fortifications with nine towers (Caernarfon Castle, Wales and Lucerne, Switzerland). It is worthy of note that in Bahá'í religion, originated in Central Asia, all temples have nine doors and domes with nine sides. The number nine is also represented in religious architecture in Armenia, as the Bagnayr Monastery and the Temple of Garni, always as the most sacred number, for it means three times the Trinity. In Bosra ash-Sham, Syria, there is a theatre fortified with nine towers around it.

7th – The above would be enough to classify that building as a unique example of modern sacred architecture. But there is more: the leitmotiv of the decorative iron pieces in art nouveau, with the tetrakys of Pythagoras, the interlacement of the triangles in octaves, the ray of creation, and the glided triangles at the capital. Furthermore, at the end of the nave there is a sculpture with two images, one dignified at the top and another curved below, which by a certain exercise of imagination can be interpreted as essence and personality.

The building was finished in 1927, so it had begun some years before, when Gurdjieff was still living at the Prieure, writing the first series of his work. Now, concerning the author or the authors of that Legominisms, who among their disciples could have participated in the design of the building?

Formulating hypotheses in a loose basis, it is known that Alexander von Salzmann had great knowledge of that kind of building, from his experience in Hellerau and before, his coexistence in Munich with Kandinsky and maybe with other exponents of Bauhaus. It is also known that Frank Lloyd Wright used to go to Munich by that early time, and they two were afterwards in France and USA, always keeping contact with Gurdjieff.

In addition, biographical notes about Gurdjieff say that Alexander "disappeared"[1] in the period around the constructions and the inauguration of the building. It seems that he was in Paris, probably working with antiquities, and he was seen sometimes alone at night, at the cafés. Little it is known and written about the life of Alexander von Salzmann. However, we have reports about his remarkable artistic training and the great familiarity he shared with the master, as well as of the phase of his disease and a certain meeting with Gurdjieff in a coffee in Avon, whose content of the conversation excites curiosities. Would Alexander have been so great to the point of actively participating in the Legominisms in total silence, maintaining a complete anonymity? Would this fact contributed for his disease and precocious death?

Carrying my suppositions on, I dare to suggest that Gurdjieff planned ahead at least the last phase of his life, with a great antecedence, considering that while he was at the Prieure he was simultaneously preparing his following phase, in which he would devote himself to classes of movements and sacred dances (see Supplementary Note).

* * *

In addition to what was written above, slides were shown at the Conference. Due to the many pauses caused by difficulties with the slides projector, questions were made during the presentation. Anne asked about Bauhaus style and commented the building is really Art Nouveau. Sy asked the price for which Salle Pleyel was sold (answer not known). About music and acoustics, Bryce told about a disk of a choral inside a church, what the angle at the temple of

---

[1] *Gurdjieff, a Biography - The Anatomy of a Myth*, James Moore, p. 236.

Luxor means – it seems to "reflect the changing angle of the pole star throughout the years of its construction".[2]

It followed that:

1. The building in subject is Salle Pleyel (a great concert hall at 252, du Faubourg Saint-Honoré, Paris, France), where Gurdjieff used to give Enneagram-based movements. It was built by Gustave Lyon, expert in acoustics, and Jean-Baptiste Mathon, architect. Up to 1937 it was managed by Credit Lyonnais (a French financial institution) and in 1998 it was sold to private owners.

2. Gurdjieff passed the year 1921 in Germany, where he tried in vain to rent the Dalcroze Institute, Festspielhaus Hellerau, near Dresden. This had been built as a "Modern Cathedral" (1912 - new concepts regarding the unity of the arts: architecture, music, dance, and theatre). Alexander von Salzmann took part in the planning.

3. Gurdjieff goes to the Prieure (Fontainebleau, France) in 1922, where he stays up to 1932, always maintaining an apartment in Paris, where he goes regularly. In this period he is also devoted to musical composition and writes his books, besides doing several trips. In 1930, A. Salzmann is seen in Paris again. Gurdjieff moves to Rue Labie and afterwards to Rue des Colonels Renard, always near Salle Pleyel.

4. Legominism[3] is a means to transmit information to future generations, somehow encrypted within objects, intentionally introducing certain INEXACTITUDES. This idea illustrates Shannon Information Theory, which states: "Entropy (chaos) is maximized when all possibilities are equally probable". In information, the less probable is the more relevant.

5. Possibly they all met before in Munich, like de Hartmann, Kandinsky and A. Salzmann. Gurdjieff may have been in Paris in advance. He could have been in Munich at the same time that all those artists and future disciples. It is possible that there were people that is not said to be in the work, but were also working for Gurdjieff. All this may have been part of a "Ludibrium"[4] – like it is also said about Jesus Christ's story, that it would have been something like a theatre play planned in advance and represented by "actors", each one playing his role, to symbolize the teachings with their own living.

---

[2] *Sacred Architecture*, A. T. Mann.
[3] "In all the productions which we shall intentionally create on the basis of this Law for the purpose of transmitting to remote generations, we shall intentionally introduce certain also lawful inexactitudes, and in these lawful inexactitudes we shall place, by means available to us, the contents of some true knowledge or other which is already in the possession of men of the present time"; *Beelzebub's Tales*, Chapter 30 (Art).
[4] *Harmonious Circle*; James Webb.

All & Everything Conference 2001

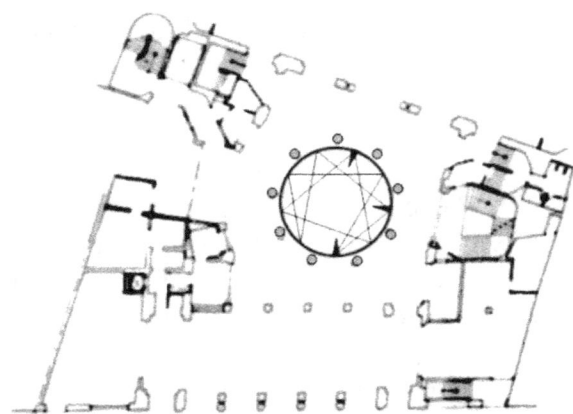

6. Daivibrizkar: "The law of the action of the vibrations arising in the atmosphere of enclosed spaces".[5] The size and form also the volume of air influence beings in particular ways. Confirming this law, among other things, we could see from the photos that in the hall where the Enneagram is, people unconsciously walk through it, now crossing and going to the centre, now stopping on the arrows or on a number of the circumference.

Supplementary Note

Before the Conference, I thought that probably Gurdjieff prepared this building especially for his classes, to give the movements over the Enneagram.

During this Conference, having asked everybody if they knew the building, I found only two participants who had been there. Prof. Thring said he went to movement classes upstairs, in common studios. Chris Thompson had been there at the age of thirteen and didn't notice anything special.

After the Conference, in Paris, I had more information. The nine columns form also "La Rotonde" at the second floor, a round room inside the ballet studios, all closed and not used. I asked three persons of the Work (M. S., J.S., A.K), and they had no idea of any Enneagram at Salle Pleyel.
My conclusion is that Gurdjieff's intention was exactly and only a Legominisms, for future generations.

© Copyright 2001 – Ana Helena Fragomeni - All Rights Reserved

---

[5] *Beelzebub's Tales*, Chapter 30 (Art).

The Psychology of Transformation

John Perrott

Good morning! Welcome to our first presentation, 'The Psychology of Transformation'.

I would like to thank briefly those who endured my presentation 2 years ago when, as was subsequently diagnosed, I had cancer and could only manage a whisper. Fortunately, as a result of radiotherapy, all is now well. I've even given up smoking - so demonstrating the essence of a traditional Sufi aphorism regarding such sacrifices, i.e. "Fear is all you need"!

As an Introduction, I'll read an extract from 'Views...' given in New York, 13 March, 1924.

For the sake of those who would retrace my steps, the following concepts in the core literature of the 4thWay, once integrated, have contributed to this presentation:

1. Static Triad - relating to possible *centres-of-gravity*

2. Three-story Factory - the (Enneagram) of *transformation*

3. Octave of Centres (the Sex-octave) - the Way of possible Ascension of man

4. Essence & Personality - what's *given* and what's *acquired*

5. Three *totalities*

6. 4 states of Consciousness - Sleep, Waking Sleep, Self and Objective consciousness

7. 5 states of 'I' - Multiplicity, Magnetic Centre, Deputy Steward, Steward and Master

Those of you who have studied 'Gurdjieff: Cosmic Secrets', by Russell Smith, will have seen that on page 45, there is presented a scheme of 13 octaves in 3 scales (not including the 'Unknown Scale') which represents the centres, the parts of centres and the parts-of-parts of centres respectively. On page 49 (un-numbered - but follows page 48) there is a 3-tiered presentation of the same data, which affords a clear recognition of the structural distinction and growth as between Essence (the given) and Personality (the acquired). I will show an integration of all seven sources - with simplified representations of centres for the sake of clarity. Gurdjieff says in 'Views...' pages 140-141 that:

> "A man should be able to give a total of 30 for everything taken together. This figure can be obtained only if each centre can give a certain corresponding number - for instance, 12 + 10 + 8."

"If 30 is correctly a true manifestation of man and this 30 is produced by three centres in a corresponding correlation, then it is imperative that the centres should be in this correlation."

Therefore, in this presentation, I will describe experiences and use terminology such as is typical of a student (the '8' of the '30') - notwithstanding that, unknown to him initially, many of them have objective origins. For example, feelings are really the 'sensations' of the 2nd totality and 'thoughts' the sensations of the 3rd. Gurdjieff tells us, again in *Views*:

"All our emotions are rudimentary forms of "something higher", e.g. fear may be an organ of future clairvoyance, anger of real force, etc."

However, at present, the aim is to describe and offer a practicable *psychology of transformation* as a framework of reference for a typical student.

(See Three-Story Factory diagram)

I intend to walk you through this diagram, of which you should all have a copy, anticipating that we will resolve any questions together during the allotted time after I have finished. However, in the event that there are problems arising from ineffective communications during the presentation, please feel free to interrupt and clarify them 'in real time'.

Additional Notes:

1. Impressions enter via the Mi-Fa interval (the "mechano-coinciding Mdnel-In") destined, for the most part, for the emotional-part (drawn attention) of this centre - the instinctive foundation of Essence. Pleasure/pain stimuli interface with basic urges towards movement, e.g. blinking, shying away, lurching, reaching, mimicking, etc. Actual causes of pleasure/pain, etc. are not known (sub-conscious polarities) because Nature only pushes things up to La - and the Intellectual part of the Emotional part of essence-centres is at Ti! (It is at the Intellectual part of the Intellectual part of the personality-centres). This, of course, applies to all centres.

2. These basic urges instigate 'follow-up' movements as functions of the drawn attention in the Moving Centre. Such basic movements gradually aggregate and become 'scripted' (in the same way as gymnastic performances). Movement is the beginning of the development of Personality and the first acquired condition of the possible attainment of Individuality.

3. Particularly strong and/or repeated impressions represent meaningful/significant data. Meaning/significance is the second condition often survival of entity (Essence) and is the true foundation of *emotion*.

4. Such repeated data stimulates memory (codification). This is the second acquired condition of the possible attainment to Individuality. It also fulfils the conditions of space/time such that everything doesn't have to happen *at once* and *in the same place*. So far, everything has gone 'to plan' (if there were actually a plan). All functions and relations between these lower centres are wholesome (as far as they go).

5. Normal development would continue with the unification of these lower centres via their integration in the midst of Life's ever-present and 'toning' vicissitudes to form the Higher Emotional Centre, were it not for the influences at '9' - arising externally. For the moment, we will continue to follow the 'normalising' sequence. As a result of the self-consciousness afforded by unification, real work-on-oneself is now possible and the La-Ti interval can begin to be traversed (Steward/Holy Planet Purgatory). Unfortunately, self-consciousness, though rare, has often been perceived as the end of the journey - subject only to (somehow) 'jumping into the arms of God'.

6. These are the results of conscientious activities resulting from *meditation and prayer* - aggregating, mapping and comparing experiences in order to distil and stimulate Objectivity and Reason. Real Stewardship - yearning for Master.

7. By the same token, one can recognise *intuition* as the 'shadow' of *contemplation*. However, the advantage will only be gained if it is not confused with uncontrolled imagination.

8. Our belief-structures (current convictions as to *meaning/significance*) will be enhanced and magnified in support of intellectual constructs sourced in Objective Reason. Simple 'beliefs' will become Faith and our works will be encouraged.

    It is not difficult to see that the possibility of a higher development cycle is now established 5-6-7-8-5.... The result is the prioritisation of existence towards the attainment of *self-individuality* - "gravity begins to flow upwards"! All significant activities are now aspects of the 2nd and 3rd Totalities - and the establishment of "a permanent passenger in the carriage" (1st Totality) is all but assured. It seems to us obvious that this is the singular aim of all relevant traditions.

9. Ironically, it is the original establishment of Reason among the few of mankind that was probably the downfall of mankind. With the establishment of Reason, man subdued Nature; a few brilliant individuals resolved problems that others copied and Life became too easy. Atlantis fell, (man fell from Grace) "Oskiano" became obsolete, education 'set in' and the reasonable were left to wonder why it was that their young people were remaining so 'dumb'. The ones that were not destroyed (as *interfering*) by the 'dumb' set themselves to solve this problem - which has probably led to most of us, being gathered here this morning. For the same reasons, initial guidance now has to be received from

external sources - until such time as the 5-6-7-8-5 cycle is re-established. We all have to traverse this phase - under the auspices of Deputy Steward.

10. Many false truths are much trickier, e.g. taking it on board that many unconscionable activities have to undertaken in order to succeed, to be happy, to be secure, etc. Sleeping man is always gullible in relation to pressure from relatively conscious man - let alone in the face of possible conscious evil.

11. We have all met with the vehement arguments in favour of the obviously false. More than anything else, it is probably just these inner contradictions that create the psychology of victim hood - the most gullible and easily influenced in society.

Clearly, as serious students, we should perceive our existence as 'work-in-progress'. As is also quite obvious – even to the unregenerate intellect (although unwelcome to the false personality), we can't begin to truly practice the Work in the absence of a self-conscious "passenger in our carriage". Until then, we are inevitably dependent upon the guidance of those who have already attained – together with whatever modicum of critical faculty and force is available. Consequently, most of our work at The Dog, both here and in the USA, focuses on guiding students in the context of Russell's book, *Cosmic Secrets*, as the effective and objective map of both the terrain and the destination. This preparation culminates in the exercise named 'April Fools', the anniversary of which, by the way, is on Sunday.

In closing, I will read a passage from *Life is Real Only Then, When "I Am"*, page 160.

Thank you for your attention and a very Happy Easter and best wishes to you all.

The Three-Story Diagram

Impressions enter from outside, via the five senses, and are recorded in the Instinctive Centre.

The Moving Centre is stimulated to function in response to these impressions.

Some incoming impressions enter with such force that their entry creates not only a corresponding reaction in the Moving Centre but also stimulates registration of them in the Emotional Centre.

Subsequent impressions registered in the Emotional Centre, which are similar to impressions previously perceived, incite memory, i.e., create a codification in the Intellectual Centre.

If a man unifies the lower Centres into Conscience, then these incoming impressions, which have been forcibly recorded in the Emotional Centre, will also begin to resound in the Higher Emotional Centre.

The accumulation of impressions that have reached the Higher Emotional Centre, if perceived correctly, will give birth to Objective Reason. For example, the Higher Mental Centre will begin to function with Impartiality and Reason.

The functioning of the Higher Mental Centre, in imparting Objective Reason to the Intellectual Centre, makes it possible for the Intellectual Centre to cognize various realities - without having to actually experience them through sensation. The creation of an intellectual construct based on the influence of perceiving Objective Reason will create, in the Emotional Centre, the corresponding belief-structure, which it must create in order to support the given intellectual model.

If a man does NOT awaken Conscience, Reason will not be imparted to his Intellectual Centre; rather, he will be conditioned only by 'false truths' (consensual reality) implanted in his Intellectual Centre from outside, thus equipping him with a false and contradictory intellectual model of reality.

These 'false truths' - false models, e.g., "Snakes are slimy!" will unfortunately invoke corresponding "false belief-structures" in his Emotional Centre which it inevitably creates to support them. Thus, False Personalities are born.

The establishment of such false belief-structures, together with accompanying emotions necessary for their support, will also condition a man's sensations and movements. Thus, if a man (manifesting from some prerequisite false personality) encounters a real snake ... and touches it, he may still believe that the snake is slimy, even though it is not. However, Gurdjieff tells us, in the following passage, that it is possible for a man to up-root these false beliefs ÿ "by centuries rooted in him" - if he understands the Laws of World-creation and World-maintenance:

Likewise, an all-round awareness of everything concerning these sacred laws also conduces, in general, to this, that three-brained beings irrespective of the form of their exterior coating, by becoming capable in the presence of all cosmic factors not depending on them and arising round about them - both the personally favourable as well as the unfavourable - of pondering on the sense of existence, acquire data for the elucidation and reconciliation in themselves of that, what is called, 'individual collision' which often arises, in general, in three-brained beings from the contradiction between the concrete results flowing from the processes of all the cosmic laws and the results presupposed and even quite surely expected by their what is called 'sane-logic'; and thus, correctly evaluating the essential significance of their own presence, they become capable of becoming aware of the genuine corresponding place for themselves in these common-cosmic actualization."

(Note from the editor: Due to the inaudibility of the tape, a transcription of the question, answers and comments is not available.)

© Copyright 2001 - John Perrott - All Rights Reserved

All & Everything Conference 2001

The Three-Story Factory Diagram
© The Dog Pub USA (modified with permission by The Dog UK)

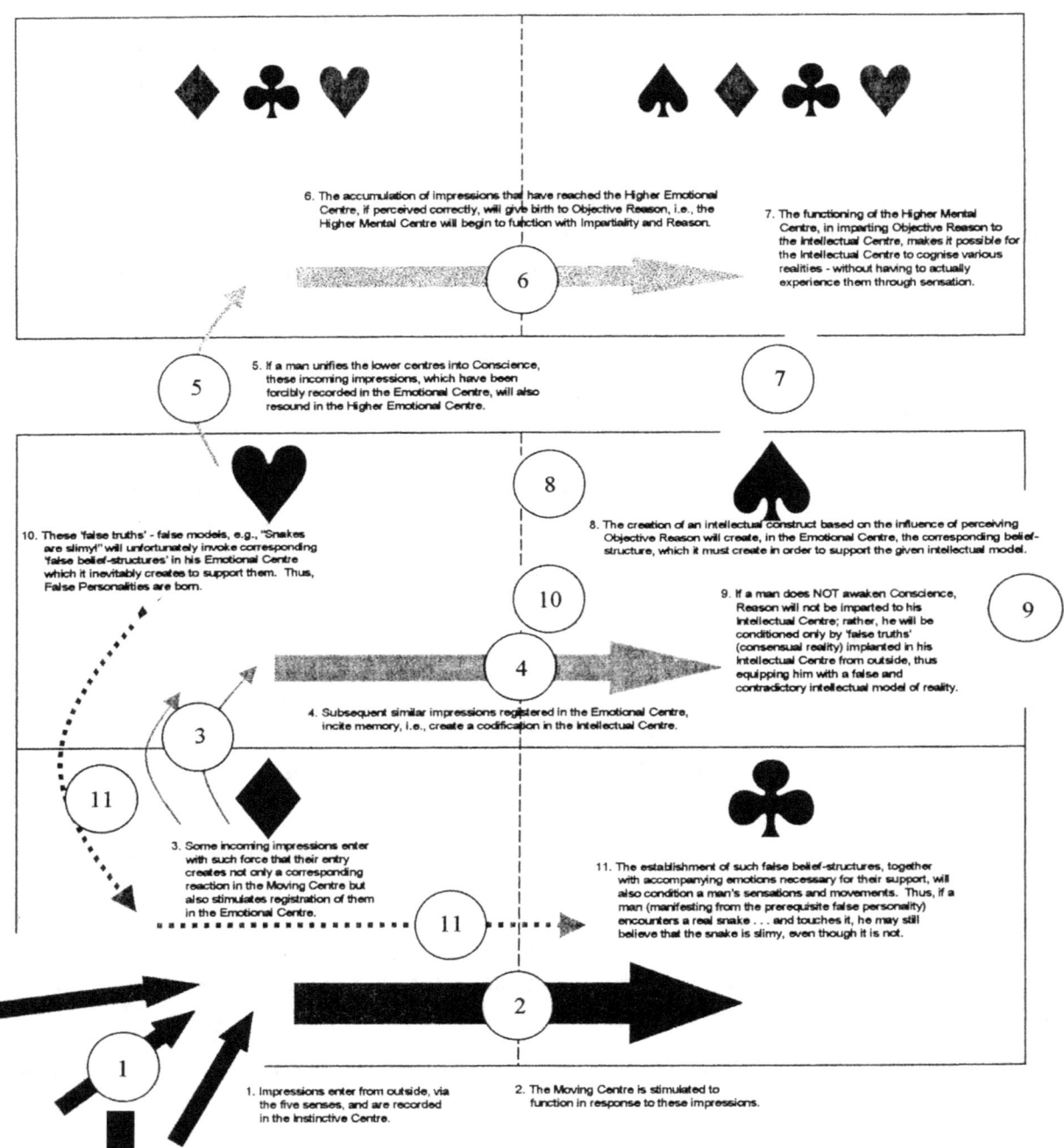

Beelzebub Restores our Understanding of Teleology and Ontology

Professor M. W. Thring

Gurdjieff is unique among 'Messengers from God' in that he wrote his own 'Book' (Biblios) and strove 'with might and main' to find the right words and the best way to 'bury the bone deep' so that no one could unearth the bone of meaning without considerable and persistent efforts. My experience is that reading it three times as G. advises is only the very beginning! I am sure that he did this in order to keep his message unspoilt, and not split into rival sects, each claiming to have the sole true interpretation, by interpreters who were, at least partially, concerned with self-promotion, in the way that has happened to some other 'Messages'.

However, my experience of meeting him several times at the end of his life, convinced me that he was anxious to bring together all those people who were studying his ideas seriously and practically, to form a single Mesoteric Nucleus; while at the same time he clearly intended All and Everything to be widely studied to bring these old Asiatic ideas to the Western World. "Take the understanding of the East and the knowledge of the West - and then seek". (Aph. 19, VRW, p274)

I must therefore strive to keep my 'interpretation', as far as I can, to bringing his ideas to bear on the problems of modern science, philosophy and metaphysics.

Modern Science is based on a set of quasi-religious dogma largely as a result of the philosophies of **Descartes** and **Francis Bacon**.

"Descartes (1596-1650) discerned in mathematics precision and certainty of the land that truly merited the title of *scientia* ...the key to making progress in the applied sciences... a kind of paradigm for all human understanding ... Descartes described the whole of philosophy as like a tree: roots metaphysics, trunk physics, branches various sciences including mechanics, morals and medicine ... we can and should achieve knowledge that is 'useful in life' and that will one day make us 'masters and possessors of nature' ....Descartes proposes to mathematicise science. The material world is simply an indefinite series of variations in the shape size and motion of the single simple homogeneous matter - *res extensa*. Under this category he includes even complex animal behaviour of purely mechanical processes... There is one class of phenomena which cannot be handled in this way -conscious experience... A dualistic theory of substance: *res extensa and res cogitans*, thinking substance which is entirely independent of matter. And each conscious individual is a unique thinking substance: "This 'I' that is, the soul by which I am what I am, is entirely distinct from the body, and would not fail to be what it is even if the body did not exist."" (Cambridge Dictionary of Philosophy, pp. 193-7)

All & Everything Conference 2001

Descartes' "Cogito Ergo Sum" regards man as a two-brained being who confines his knowledge to purely logical deductions from his sensory observations. He ignores our emotions such as Love, Intuition and Understanding with all their power of perceiving the greater part of Reality which is not directly perceptible to our senses, but which includes the interconnectedness and meaning of everything. He puts everything we perceive with our senses on the same level, thus destroying Ontology. This has led to the ridiculous consequence that a number of scientists are seeking **a mathematical 'theory of everything'**. They try to fit all Reality into the Procrustean Bed of mathematics.

Gurdjieff insists that man has the possibility of becoming a three-brained or three-centred being: "In all my three 'being centres'- namely in the three centres localised in the presence of every three centred being, and which exist under the names of 'Thinking', 'Feeling' and 'Moving' centres..." (A&E p. 163)

1. The brain predetermined by Great Nature for the concentration and further actualising of the first holy force - Holy-Affirming - is localised and found in the head.
2. The second brain ... Holy-Denying is placed in their common presences along the whole of their back in what is called the 'spinal column'.
3. The place of concentration and source for the further manifestation of the third holy force. ...Holy Reconciling.... Most of the separate parts of this being brain are localised in the region of their breast, they call this totality the 'Solar Plexus'." (A&E p.p. 146-7)

"When these favourites of yours completely ceased consciously to actualise in their common presences the 'being-Partkdolg-duty', thanks only to the results of which what is called sane **'comparative mentation'** as well as the possibility of conscious active manifestation can arise in beings from various associations ... the time when their separate 'brains' associating now quite independently..." (A&E p.p. 480-1)

Descartes' philosophy of observation and intellectual reasoning fails completely to take account of the Holy-Reconciling which should be provided by the Feeling Centre. This leads him to irreconcilable Dualism, and to **the ideas that Reality is limited to what can be observed with our senses.** Since we can distinguish different levels of Being only with our feelings, his philosophy puts everything on the same level and Ontology is meaningless. Ontology: "the branch of metaphysics that deals with the nature of being." (Collins Dictionary)

Hence for Descartes and for most modern scientists:

"The 18th personal commandment of our COMMON CREATOR which declared: 'Love everything that breathes'." (A&E p. 198) is meaningless verbiage.

For eighty years theoretical Physicists have been trying to find a mathematical equation which would embrace the forces of electromagnetism, nuclear forces and Gravitation in a single formula. They are no nearer than we were in 1949 when JG Bennett, RL Brown and I published a paper in which we attempted to fit both gravitation and electromagnetism into a single five-dimensional framework!

I think the reason for this failure to find a 'theory-of-everything' is given in a paragraph from *Fragments* (ISM. pp 304-5). Ouspensky had spoken about Kant's ideas of phenomena and noumena and G says 'If Kant had introduced **the idea of scale** into his arguments many things he wrote would be very valuable.' I have come to the conclusion that, because Gravity is only important on the macroscopic scale >> kilograms while nuclear forces and photons (light in its particle aspect) are important on the micro scale of Planck's constant (6.6×10^{-34} joule-seconds), the attempt to find a single formula will always fail. "The difference between each of them and our common great Megalocosmos is only in scale". (A&E p775)

The most extreme example of this ignoring of Ontology is the 'Reductionists' or 'Nothing-Butters' who say that a man is 'nothing but' a highly ordered collection of molecules each following automatically the laws of physics and chemistry! They think therefore that everything can be found out about the working of an animal or a plant by cutting it up and studying the pieces!

Francis Bacon destroyed the perception of Meaning and Purpose for his followers, by saying that it was idle to look for purpose in Nature. He thus made Teleology a forbidden subject. He also limited our understanding of Reality to observations that can be repeated by others at will, thus forbidding scientists to believe in any paranormal events.

"Teleology: a) the study of the evidence of design or purpose in nature, b) the ultimate purpose of things, esp. natural processes, c) the belief that final causes exist. Biology: the belief that natural phenomena have a predetermined purpose." (Collins Dictionary)

"Francis Bacon (1561-1626) claimed all knowledge as his province and advocated new ways by which men could establish a legitimate command over nature.... About 1591 Robert Devereux, third Earl of Essex, a favourite of Queen Elizabeth, became his patron. By 1600, however, Bacon was the Queen's learned counsel and in 1601 he drew up a report denouncing Essex as a traitor....With the accession of James I in 1603, Bacon sought anew to gain influence... He was engaged in a series of conflicts with Sir Edward Coke in an effort to safeguard the royal prerogative... After a succession of legal posts he was appointed Lord Chancellor ... in 1618. Between 1608 and 1620 he prepared at least 12 drafting's of... ***Novum Organum***. Bacon fell from power in 1621 following charges of bribery." (Encyclopedia. Britanaca, I, p. 715)

I feel that this record does not qualify him to be regarded as the **ethical adviser** of scientists.

"The founding principles of science were laid out with clarity and wit by **Francis Bacon** the 'father' of our discipline. Bacon's view of the purpose of science was clear; that by wing inductive experimentation (the Novum Organum in contrast to the deductive operations of philosophy) substantial improvements in knowledge could be made for the physical benefit of humanity....The simple and overriding moral principle of science is that a researcher must seek to use scientific knowledge for the explicit benefit of humanity (not in the interests of this living system that is so much bigger than us or any other such quasi-spiritual gibberish) .... Bacon does not recognise the existence of limits to scientific knowledge whether they are prescribed by Aristotle, by the schoolmen or by a man who lives in a converted watermill." (R.G.A. Faragher, *Science and Public Affairs*, Feb 2001 p. 27)

"Bacon championed the new empiricism resulting from the achievements of early modem science... The goal of acquiring knowledge is the good of mankind- Knowledge is power. Bacon thought that we must **intervene in nature, manipulating it by means of experimental control**, leading to the invention of new technology. There are well-known hindrances to acquisition of knowledge of causal laws... such hindrances Bacon calls 'idols'. Idols of the tribe are natural mental tendencies, **among which are the searches for purposes in nature,** and the impulse to read our own desires and needs into nature... Bacon held that nothing exists in nature except bodies (material objects) acting in conformity with fixed laws." (Cambridge Dictionary of Philosophy p. 60)

Thus the legacy of **Bacon,** too many scientists is that:
- The only purpose of science is to help man for immediate short-term local-group aims to enslave Mother Nature, Gaia, Organic Life.
- There are no purposes in nature
- Reality is limited to what we can perceive directly with our senses
- Scientific theory is only important if it leads to results of practical use as well as being experimentally verifiable.

'All and Everything' can give us an understanding of the meaning and purpose of human life and of the possibility given to all three-brained beings to help the purpose of our FATHER CREATOR, provided they make enough 'Conscious Labours' and undergo enough 'Intentional Suffering'. It also gives clear expositions of levels of Being.

Beelzebub Restores Teleology

The Supreme Mystery is expressed in the words:

"Our ENDLESSNESS was forced to create the whole World which now exists at the present time.... OUR CREATOR OMNIPOTENT once ascertained that this same Sun Absolute, on which HE dwelt with HIS cherubim and seraphim, was, although almost imperceptibly yet nevertheless gradually, diminishing in volume. (A&E pp. 748-9)

The choice of the word OMNIPOTENT is clearly intentional to bring out the paradox:

"During this review our OMNIPOTENT CREATOR for the first time made it clear that the cause of this gradual diminishing of the Sun Absolute was merely the Heropass, that is, the flow of Time itself....if the Heropass should so continue to diminish the volume of the Sun Absolute, then sooner or later, it would ultimately bring about the complete destruction of this sole place of HIS Being.... our ENDLESSNESS was then just compelled to take certain corresponding measures, so that from this Heropass the destruction of our Most Most Holy Sun Absolute could not eventually occur." (A&E p. 749)

"our ALL-MAINTAINING ENDLESSNESS decided to change the principle of the system of functioning of both of these fundamental sacred laws, and, namely, HE decided to make their independent functioning dependent on forces coming from outside." (A&E p.p. 752-3)

"for this new system of functioning of the forces which had until then maintained the existence of the Most Most Holy Sun Absolute, there were required outside of the Sun Absolute corresponding sources in which such forces could arise and from which they could flow into the presence of the Most Most Holy Sun Absolute, our ALMIGHTY ENDLESSNESS was just then compelled to create our now existing Megalocosmos with all the cosmoses of different scales and relatively independent cosmic formations present in it, and from then on the system which maintained the existence of the Sun Absolute began to be called Trogoautoegocrat". (A&E p. 753)

This statement that the 15 Billion year old Universe perceived by scientists was intentionally created out of nothingness as a living self-maintaining Being to resist the destruction caused by the flow of Time is far beyond logical understanding. However, it can have an enormous effect on our feelings if we ponder on it enough -if The Whole Universe was made for a Great Purpose then surely our **ability to ponder must have been given to us so that we have a chance to make some tiny contribution to its maintenance.**

So what do we learn from A&E about the contribution that individuals can make by 'conscious labours and intentional suffering'.

Here again we come to a supreme Mystery:

"There is localised in the head of each one of them... A concentration of corresponding cosmic substances, all the functioning of which exactly corresponds to all those functions and purposes which our Most Most Holy Protocosmos has and fulfils for the whole of the Megalocosmos. This localisation which is concentrated in their head, they call the 'head-brain'... The 'cells-of-the-head-brain', actualise for the whole presence of each of them exactly such a purpose as is fulfilled at the present time by the 'higher-perfected-bodies' of three-brained beings from the whole of our Great Universe, who have already united themselves with the Most Most Holy Sun Absolute or Protocosmos." (A&E p 777-78)

I wish to compare this Mystery with a statement by Schrödinger (Nobel Prize winning Physicist - 1933) in his *book What is Life?* (Published 1943)

"The mystics of many centuries, independently, yet in perfect harmony with each other (somewhat like the particles in an ideal gas) have described, each of them, the unique experience of his or her life in terms which can be condensed in the phrase: DEUS FACTUS SUM (I have become God)." (p. 88).

"Your nose and the organs connected with it are so adapted that you may take in and transform in your self those World-substances which there are coated in the three-brained beings similar to yourself both higher being bodies, on one of which rests the hope of our COMMON ALL-EMBRACING CREATOR for help in His needs, for the purpose of actualizations foreseen by Him for the good of everything existing." (A&E p 194)

The fourth 'being-obligolnian-striving':
"The striving from the beginning of their existence to pay for their arising and their individuality as quickly as possible, in order afterwards to be free to lighten as much as possible the Sorrow of our COMMON FATHER". (A&F p 386).

"Created with the possibility of coating in your presence that "Higher-Sacred" for the possible arising of which the whole of our now existing world was just created. (A&E p. 195)

"Love everything that breathes." (A&E p. 198)

"Love one another and God will love you". (A&E p. 1063)

These quotations show the supreme role that three brained beings can play in the Universe **if they develop their potentialities**. However, the same development that is so valuable for the maintenance of the Universe is **self**-perfection so it provides a **personal aim** in life.

"To possess the right to the name of "man", one must be one. And to be such, one must first of all, with an indefatigable persistence and an unquenchable impulse of desire, issuing from all the separate independent parts constituting one's entire common presence, that is to say with a desire issuing simultaneously from thought feeling and organic instinct, work on an all-round knowledge of oneself - at the same time struggling unceasingly with one's subjective weaknesses - and then afterwards, taking one's stand upon the results thus obtained by one's consciousness alone, concerning the defects in one's established subjectivity as well as the elucidated means for the possibility of combating them, strives for their eradication without mercy towards oneself." (A&E p.1209).

That individual men could play a role in stopping war if a number ("Two hundred conscious people", ISM p310) developed themselves to liberate enough Askokin is shown in the following quotation:

"So, when it appeared that the instinctive need for conscious labour and intentional suffering in order to be able to take in and transmute in themselves the sacred substances Abrustdonis and

Beelzebub Restores our Understanding of Teleology and Ontology

Helkdonis and thereby to liberate the sacred Askokin for the maintenance of the Moon and Anulios had finally disappeared from their psyche, then Great Nature Herself was constrained to adapt herself to extract this sacred substance by other means, one of which is precisely that terrifying process thereof reciprocal destruction." (A&E p. 1106)

The Restoring of Ontology

Some Scientists regard humans as having a higher **quality of Being** than a worm, although the majority would regard the phrase Quality of Being as meaningless. Extreme Reductionists consider us to be 'nothing more than' a more complicated pattern of molecules than the worm or the bacterium. Nearly all scientists **reject the ideas that**:

1. Everything in the Universe is interconnected into a single whole which is LIVING in the sense that it maintains itself against the increase of Entropy (Loss of Order) with Time.
2. There is a scale of Being in the Universe with this single whole at the Highest point.
3. There can exist in the Universe beings with a higher level of Being and Consciousness than man some of which we can perceive as Planets, Stars and Galaxies.
4. Individual humans can have very different levels of Being.
5. There are forms of matter or energy which are on a higher level than those detectable by any scientific instruments.
6. Human consciousness is similarly a form of energy higher than those recognisable by science such as electric currents or movement of the molecules in the brain.
7. Human consciousness has several Qualitatively different levels
8. It will always be impossible to make an artefact which has all the powers of a human which include the faculties of genuine originality and genuine love.

I think that the following quotations provide a clearly defined Ontological System of Levels of Being, Consciousness, Materiality and Energy.

G. writes:

"To me, a trifling particle of the whole of the GREAT WHOLE." (A&E p. 353)

"Every form of "life" has its own total of vibrations proper to it, which represents the totality of all the vibrations engendered from the various definite organs of the given form of life, and this total varies at different times in each form of life and depends on how intensely these variously caused vibrations are transformed by the corresponding sources or organs. Now all these heterogeneous and variously caused vibrations always blend within the limits of the whole life in the general subjective "chord of vibrations" of the given life....**Among men of recent times very many are to be met who have not as great a number of vibrations of their common presence as the number shown by the presence of the dog**. This has come about because in most of these people, one function, for instance the function of emotion, which actualizes the main quantity of subjective vibrations, is already almost completely atrophied. (A&E p. 904).

"The Omnipresent- Okidanokh obtains its prime arising in space outside of the Most Holy Sun Absolute, from the blending of these three independent forces into one, and during its further involutions it is correspondingly changed, in respect of what is called the 'Vivifyingness of Vibrations' according to its passage through what are called the 'Stopinders' or 'gravity centres' of the fundamental 'common-cosmic sacred Heptaparaparshinokh'." (A&E p. 139).

"Every 'relatively independent concentration' they then defined by the word 'cosmos' and to distinguish the different orders of arising of these 'cosmoses' they added to this definition 'cosmos' a separate corresponding name:

'The Most Most Holy Prime Source Sun Absolute itself- Protocosmos.

Each newly arisen 'Second-order-Sun' with all its consequent definite results –'Defterocosmos'.

'Third-order-Suns', i.e., those we now call 'planets', they called 'Tritocosmos'.
The smallest 'relatively independent formation' on the planets which arose thanks to the new inherency of the fifth stopinder of the sacred Heptaparaparshinokh and which is the very smallest similarity to the whole, was called Microcosmos', and, finally, those formations of the 'Microcosmos' and which also became concentrated on the planets, this time thanks to the second-order cosmic law called 'mutual attraction of the similar', were named 'Tetartocosmoses'." (A&E p.p. 759-60)

"He had attained the Reason of the Sacred Podkoolad, the last gradation before the Reason of the sacred Anklad, which is the highest to which in general any being can attain, being the third in degree from the Absolute Reason of HIS ENDLESSNESS HIMSELF. (A&E p. 1177).

"That still now existing sacred 'Determinator-of-Reason' which is applied for the determination of the gradations or, more exactly, the 'totality-of-self-awareness' of all large and small cosmic concentrations and by which not only are the gradations of their Reason measured, but there is also determined the 'degree-of-justification-of-the-sense-and-aim-of-their-existence' and also the further role of each separate individual in relationship to everything existing in our great Megalocosmos. This sacred determinator of 'pure Reason' is nothing else than a kind of measure, i.e. a line divided into equal parts; one end of this line is marked as the total absence of any Reason, i.e. absolute 'firm-calm', and at the other end there is indicated absolute Reason, i.e., the Reason of our INCOMPARABLE CREATOR ENDLESSNESS... In every three-brained being in general, irrespective of the place of his arising and the form of his exterior coating there can be crystallised data for three independent kinds of being-mentation, the totality of the engendered results of which expresses the gradations of his Reason. Data for these three kinds of being-Reason are crystallised in the presence of each three-brained being depending upon how much by means of 'being-Partkdolg duty' the corresponding higher being parts are coated and perfected in them, which should without fail compose their common presences as a whole. The first highest kind of being-Reason is the 'pure' or objective Reason which is proper to the presence of a higher being-body." (A&E pp769-70)

Beelzebub Restores our Understanding of Teleology and Ontology

"Objective Reason, which should be in the common presences of three-brained beings of all natures and all external forms, and which, in itself, is nothing else but the 'representative-of-the-Very-Essence-of-Divinity'." (A&E p. 815)

I rest my case.

Prof M. W. Thring. FREng. Sc.D.
Bell Farm, Brundish, Suffolk

© Copyright 2001 - M. W. Thring - All Rights Reserved

Beelzebub Restores our Understanding of Teleology and Ontology - Questions & Answers

Q. Professor Thring, at the beginning you said that it would not be possible in your view for scientists to come up with a theory of everything which they are trying to work at the present time, a unified theory. There is something called 'string theory' that has been around for about ten years and not verified in any way but it struck me and I am not a scientist [that it is] based on the vibratory rate of very microscopic, sub microscopic [sub-molecular] particles of various dimensions and I thought that that might actually fit in with the idea that was spoken of at the end where Gurdjieff both G and Ouspensky said 'even God can be weighed and measured' and the theory and the idea from the absolute calm… [interrupted]

Prof. Thring: The spectrum, I like to call it a spectrum.

Q. [resumed] So might it not be possible whether it is string theory or perhaps something else that they actually come up with something that would encompass all of these things including being…not just...

Prof. Thring: No, no it isn't possible because Being is something spiritual not something that physicists' can ever get hold of. Being may result in an action [unclear] reactions they can get a hold of but Being itself belongs to the part of reality which is not directly perceptible by our senses therefore it is not within the field of the physical sciences. What I am saying is that, the whole point of this is that there is much more to reality than the physical sciences can accept because they only accept things that they can weigh and measure. Therefore things like love don't come into science. Are you happy with that?

Q. I don't disagree with that but I'm wondering if science could come to a point where theory could encompass those things because Gurdjieff tells us that everything is vibrations, to the densest to the rarest.

Prof. Thring: Sex is part of mechanics.

Q. Yes, Exactly and that would include, I presume things like Being, like Love that are not regarded...

Prof. Thring: Ah, they are not the kind of vibrations that you can ever detect as vibrations you can only detect them emotionally. This is my point. The terms of reference of the physical sciences exclude the greater part of reality. Such as things like [unclear; possibly - the feeling that you do not want to die like a dog?] there is no room for that in science, the feeling that there is a purpose in the Universe, there is no room for that in science.

Beelzebub Restores our Understanding of Teleology and Ontology - Questions & Answers

Question about [Hadji Asvatz-Troov]

Prof. Thring: Yes, I know that's symbolic! Isn't it? It is symbolic.

Bert Sharp: [unclear]

Prof. Thring: That's a very good result, I agree with you.

Bert Sharp: [unclear]

Prof. Thring: Certainly, the vibrations are the lowest, and the emotional effect of that music produced an 'observer'.

Bert Sharp: Ah!

Prof. Thring: And it is only our emotional brain that can have a perception of this kind of reality. That is why religions have always existed because people have emotional visions; they want to explore this kind of reality.

Q: Hadji-Troov speaks in the quotation that you mention here... 'that the near total atrophy of the function of emotion is what diminished the totality of vibrations that he takes the measure of well, would you say in relation to the physical sciences which seem to be pretty incontrovertibly true [unclear] however where applied to the biological sciences as we have seen them unfold in the last 25-30 years I think we are seeing emerging more and more clearly a clear recognition of the enormous importance of the emotional world as a major qualifier of our humanity and of our ability to think and to think clearly too.

Prof. Thring: Do you mean the negative emotions?

Answer: No I am thinking about the normal function. I am talking about perhaps an analogue to Anulios. We are discovering that in the biological sciences there is something of great substance and of great measurability, great measurability especially in the patterns of relationship that are beginning to be understood as incontrovertibly a substrate for normalcy. And I think that the more this pursuit has been going on in the biological sciences this will unfold a different perspective of what science is capable of.

Prof. Thring: Well of course Ouspensky had the emotional brain divided into six parts didn't he? [unclear aside] But the point is the Higher parts of the emotional centre we just don't have, we don't feel proper emotions.

Answer: That's my point. I think we are beginning to discover and verify through evolutionary biology as well as through neurobiological studies how our brain is put together and how it works. The absolute essentiality of normal emotions and long before we can talk about higher emotions we are still ourselves bereft of normal emotions. We have first to rediscover that. And I believe we are in the process of really giving that a dimension that was not possible.

Prof. Thring: I think the, I like the Horse, Carriage and Driver analogy about this. We have a poor broken down horse it has never been educated and it doesn't obey the reins and it wearily drags the cart around. Meanwhile the driver may well not be sitting in the driving seat and we have got a rather broken down cart. We need a horse otherwise we wouldn't get out of bed in the morning. Why should we do anything? If we hadn't a horse [unclear] at the same time these are not proper emotions. Whereas the feeling that brings one to feeling [unclear] that is a proper emotion.

Comment: Continuing Keith's ideas, which I agree with, The Centre for Disease Control the United States and I think all of their major cancer hospitals teaching centres do acknowledge today that the person who is fighting cancer who has religion an/or has a circle of love to support them have almost twice the chance of beating their cancer. So here we have MD Doctors, scientists acknowledging some of higher emotional centres, maybe they are not using the terminology we who study Gurdjieff would like them to use but I'd like to think it is a very good beginning.

Prof. Thring: Oh there is tremendous psychosomatic affect of the feelings on getting well. There is no question about that. The normal thing in people who are going to die is that they do not want to die.

Comment: Could I just that the acknowledging the lady is talking about is not done scientifically it is done from the other perceptive qualities of the human being. In other words when the physician and the scientist acknowledges something of an emotional kind, possibly even spiritual, he is not actually scientific, he is acknowledging other things outside his sphere of the kind that the lecturer is referring to. But he has the humility to recognize that human beings are more than the materialistic paradigm of the scientist.

Comment: I'd like to think that I have had the pleasure of meeting some of them. These very, very dedicated Doctors are not doing as you say, they are going a little beyond it. First of all there are exact statistics that have been done on this subject. It is documented and I don't think that they say [I am quoting John? from the University of Pittsburgh] they don't say well, this is another area I don't understand or don't deal with. I've heard John say 'Aren't we fortunate to have this extra help?'

Prof. Thring: What we are fortunate to have is that we have in us not completely destroyed the crude rudiments for a conscience. That's where we are fortunate. Because we have that, we recognize our sense of the sacred which has nothing to do with science, the sense of the sacred. And the vibrations you find in an old Cathedral where people have worshiped for hundreds of years has nothing to do with science and we also have, and this is very important, we have a feeling in us that we have been given life and we owe a bit of a debt for it. These are real feelings,

Beelzebub Restores our Understanding of Teleology and Ontology - Questions & Answers

the feeling that somehow we must repay for the privilege of being here in life. We do have these feelings but they don't play a very big role in our lives.

Comment: [unclear - Try to imagine what it would be like if you had never been born]

Prof. Thring: The word sacred is important to me. The word sacred deserves the recognition of physical science.

[unclear]

Prof. Thring: Well after all it is really the saying of all the mystics, 'I have become God' which is obviously a very sacred experience of the very highest [order] and they only say 'I have become God' while in a mystical state, not for the rest of their lives.

[unclear]

Question: When you said, Professor Thring, science has excluded its, say feeling, being and all this, it has limited itself, it is limited...

Prof. Thring: To sensory observations.

Question: Would that mean science is destructive?

Prof. Thring: If it says as Bacon said 'That's all there is' then it is destructive. In fact Bacon's science is now destroying the world, isn't it? Cutting down the rain forest, the exhaustion of fish we are every kind of thing to make sure our descendants won't have a decent world to live in. a because we are applying Bacon's science. Bacon's science is, the main purpose of science is to get what we want from Mother Nature.

Comment: I just wanted to know [unclear]

Question: What do you see as a route for healing science?

Prof. Thring: [long pause] I would say it is spiritual, really, that is all I can say about it, it is spiritual.

Question: Do you see anything that one could think of in terms of steps on the rung? You write books but mostly you are saying things are not right. How can we cure the situation?

Prof. Thring: ...to ponder to the point where we could begin to get a deeper understanding. I mean pondering is meditation, or there are lots of words, opening oneself I think that this is getting away from the personality that blocks everything.

Question: Here we are all convinced and we have no problem with what you are saying. I'm wondering how you have foreseen possibilities.

Prof. Thring: Quite honestly I fear this; that until the disaster has become obvious to everybody we will not do anything about it and that humanity may very well destroy its own [nest?] It is a very real danger. But I do feel that Gurdjieff's teaching and some other people [unclear, possibly that have a conscience?] are the only hope and I feel that Gurdjieff was a very powerful man. His ideas are really worked on by conscious labours and intentional suffering.

Question: This still leaves me with the question about Hadji-Troov. Hadji is referred to as 'the greatest scientist' and how he comes to be that and is recognized as that is laid out beautifully in the chapter. This is a real personal evolution through Hadji's life, where he comes to a very tractable and real realisation of each of the brains, his journeys stepwise through the physical, loco motor, the emotional and the intellectual and finally he steps beyond that and it seems to me [to be] so well stepped out and all of this with an aim for scientific inquiry, I don't want to let you off the hook as far as the science is concerned because I think it is so very important. I think Gurdjieff has placed this and underscored it...

Prof. Thring: Yes but he uses the word 'science' in a different sense from the sense that modern scientists use. That's the point. Gurdjieff's 'science' is all knowledge, which is what the original meaning of the word was but modern science is limited to what you can perceive with your senses.

Response: Ah! But he does say that precisely -verifiable- This is, is the whole business of vibrations.

Prof. Thring: Yes but verifiable is a different matter, some things can only be verified emotionally, such as the existence of God.

Comment: It just does seem to be what Hadji is pointing to, for me.

Comment: I am interested in this subject. What Hadji was saying, for me anyway [is], that vibrations can be measured. If I play a chord of G minor on the piano it has certain vibrations that can be measured but in order to really experience that vibration I myself have to become a chord of G minor because I cannot experience that vibration if I am sitting there in this cave with all my thoughts and feelings and all my analytical apparatus and my categorizations I will never experience the chord of G minor. So what Hadji is saying for me anyway [is] that I play this piano and if I am in the right condition I can experience this piano and the vibrations that are coming from it. And that implies to me that I must be in a state of objectivity and impartiality in order to have that experience. But I cannot have that experience if my mind is trying to analyze what the chord of G minor is, because I'll never experience this.

Seminar 1 - Chapters 3, 4 & 5 of Beelzebub's Tales to His Grandson

Facilitator: Sophia Wellbeloved

(An impromptu summary of Chapter Three was given by members of the seminar. The points raised during the seminar have been summarised below, mostly using participants' own words, but without distinguishing between the speakers. Some contributions were inaudible.)

This chapter may be autobiographical material. If we translate the dates given to earth dates they correspond to points in Gurdjieff's life.

This is difficult to calculate because there are different times referred to in the *Tales*. Also Gurdjieff's dates have been shown by Paul Taylor to be symbolic rather than historical.

It is important to note that Hassein was glad.

Gurdjieff brings in Mullah Nassr Eddin, his popular sayings are wise and humorous, this is an introduction of humour in the material. There is also a point on p. 69 about egoism. This may be a warning to point out the danger of inflation due to higher psychological knowledge.

Who is the captain and who is Beelzebub?

The captain appears in several chapters. Though he is not in many chapters, which may be symbolic for the chapters in which he appears. Also it is symbolic: how polite these conversations are, there is great courtesy.

The captain also represents common sense. I see the whole book as a how to, what to avoid. The decision [to wait] makes sense, because of the forces more powerful than I am, it is common sense to submit to those forces. Submission also occurs in the Koran, it means I accept the conditions of my life and I submit to what has been given.

The captain presents the options to Beelzebub impartially, he doesn't express an opinion.

That was the first meeting with Zilnotrago, do you connect any other chapter to this? Yes, It has to do with risk. Next time round [chapter 35] Beelzebub wants to go to the planet Deskaldino. To get there, there is a whole solar system of Zilnotrago to go through. But, there is an intention for the change of course, and so they go straight through.

All & Everything Conference 2001

Why is Zilnotrago cyanic acid?

Actually from the footnote it says that Zilnotrago is a special gas, which is similar to cyanic acid. Gurdjieff is deliberately not saying it is cyanic acid. The spirit of the book means we should not pin special labels, we are being guided to a feeling mental appreciation of something.

He is teaching us in parables not in fact. But why did he suggest that particular gas? Cyanide is a very poisonous material, but it is something 'special' and 'similar'. Gurdjieff uses new words, made up words, it gives us space for interpretation and for questioning.

Cyanic acid is extremely toxic, it affects us instantaneously, but it smells pleasant, like almonds.

Gas represents thoughts; water represents emotion. Gas is intangible, I cannot get hold of it. With lots of thoughts going on in my head it is not a good time to work on myself

So the acid is deadly? No because its effect is temporary. They wait until it is blown away. It is volatised, another air association. Zilnotrago is also connected to air in the second octave. At each interval the external source may be good or bad. If bad we must wait.

To go back to the captain, the captain appears here and he also appears in the change of course chapter, and he also appears at the end. He is not actually present when Beelzebub describes the planets or about the higher being bodies, he is never privy to these discussions, because he has his own concerns with the ship. It is when he disappears that Hassein and Beelzebub have their dialogue. The captain is not on the same level as Hassein. But that causes a difficulty, because Ahoon is also not on the same level, yet he is privy to discussions.

The respect here goes in both directions, from the captain to Beelzebub and also from Beelzebub to the captain. He gives the captain his due and leaves the running of the ship up to him, but Beelzebub is responsible for where the ship goes, the aim.

This may represent the relationship between the moving centre and the higher mental centre.

In accepting forces higher than our own we must do so 'with reverence, and at the same time praising and glorifying the wonderful and providential works of Our Lord Creator.' I am not always aware of higher forces. How do you acknowledge forces higher than your own?

There is a useful passage in 'Form and Sequence' (pp. 1171-2) 'in order that the 'planetary body of a being' may correctly serve its chief part, that is to say, in order that this auxiliary part of the whole being should properly serve his essence itself; this essence must always be just and make demands on it only according to its inherent possibilities.' It seems to me that this is similar t4 the relationship between the captain and Beelzebub.

Seminar 1 - Chapters 3, 4 & 5 of Beelzebub's Tales to His Grandson

The fact that there is something flowing in each direction is a theme in this chapter, and others, of energy, and light going in both directions.

Natural phenomena can be viewed as higher forces, there are many events in life which we humans unwisely involve ourselves in. Does that include war? No. In this context natural phenomena, like living on a volcanic island: when things get hot you get out of the way.

[After a few minutes discussion between people sitting near each other, we looked at issues which had arisen, or omitted in the previous discussion.]

In relation to the earlier point, about not opposing forces higher than our own, for me when I first encountered this teaching there were a lot of things that I would put up to oppose it, my opinions and ideas. I think this is giving me guidance on how to take a look for a while, to listen to what is being said or written.

Referring to events issuing from above, there is a lot of gladness and joy in this chapter.

We normally think we can do, do something about this. We react as a defence. This passage is saying what we have to do sometimes is be receptive in an active kind of way, not to submit in resignation but with joy and praise and glorifying the providence. But we are not always ready to have those lessons because we think we know what to do.

Gurdjieff's advice about what to do here is different from in the other chapter [chapter 35] where there is Zilnotrago. Because Hassein has grown, he is able to sustain any kind of external forces. In Chapter Three it is the beginning, things are much more delicate, fragile. When I begin the work everything is so fragile it would be like trying to feed the baby steak, which he couldn't digest it.

Who is it that grew?

Something happens to the captain. It is the captain who recognises the situation not Beelzebub. Maybe we have to be respectful of something that recognises the situation, the problem. One of the later chapters says that we have lost the instinctive ability to recognise danger.

If Gurdjieff puts the same set of ideas about the captain and Zilnotrago in different chapters it makes sense to compare them. In the later chapter the captain does not submit to the higher forces, he says he will find a way to deal with the situation. It is very difficult to examine this chapter without looking at the chapter it relates to. Because if you look at this chapter and say 'this is what Gurdjieff advises', it is only what he advises now. In other chapters under similar circumstances he advises something else. This applies to the whole book.

There is an appropriate time for everything. In the beginning they need to conserve, energy, but later they can transform energy.

All & Everything Conference 2001

I was looking at this chapter in relation to Oskiano, this is the beginning of the end of Hassein's Oskiano. The previous chapter was about the cosmic fall, but this chapter is picking up the beginning of Hassein's education. This is why the mention of egoism, and Ahoon referring to Hassein as a growing egoist, is important. Hassein has been educated to a certain point and now this is his finishing Oskiano and all Beelzebub's past, in his stories, are what Hassein has to submit to and gladly listen to and take in. I think the comet could represent the entry point of egoism in the life of every developing person, which generally comes at the age of puberty. That is what Beelzebub's stories are, to by pass this in Hassein, to give him a proper education.

This is something that is going to happen to Hassein, but at this point he is just chattering away. But he has a sharp rebuke to Ahoon, he defends himself very well.

Hassein represents the readers, all of us, and these are our characteristics - defending ourselves, a lot of chatter. But Beelzebub agrees with him. He does not condemn Hassein, he rewards him.

He listens affectionately and with a smile at the chatter of his favourite. Beelzebub is not saying Hassein is an egoist but is just coming off his lower intellect, the ordinary mind.

I think Beelzebub recognises Hassein as being a child, which he should be at this age. But Hassein made a very good assessment of the situation, he explained why he wasn't an egoist, why listening to the stories was not selfish.

Maybe Hassein is essence and Ahoon is personality?

I have a feeling that the three personages in the book are all aspects of essence, I don't think Ahoon is personality in relation to Hassein.

Perhaps Beelzebub is the embodiment of reason, the higher mental centre. Hassein is the one who is learning, the intellectual centre needs to receive reason in order to create the basis for objective consciousness. Ahoon plays the part of self-consciousness, or higher emotional centre. The captain could represent the emotional centre, the way he points out danger. There is a significance with his father becoming a ruler. This would suggest the higher emotional centre.

It is a knotty problem about who they are, and it probably won't be solved; but there is a hint contained in what happens at the end of the story, because Ahoon is not transformed, through no fault of his own, whereas Hassein has been transformed and Beelzebub as well

Where, in the book, has Hassein been transformed? Hassein is transformed and Beelzebub says specifically how he is transformed, in the passage after Beelzebub has been transformed when Hassein weeps. Hassein becomes Beelzebub's future substitute, and the people of planet Earth} become his people.

Ahoon is depicted as Beelzebub's memory.

Seminar 1 - Chapters 3, 4 & 5 of Beelzebub's Tales to His Grandson

Ahoon represents my emotional centre, undeveloped emotional centre, which needs education.

Ahoon represents my body, Ahoon always accompanies Beelzebub on his visits to earth.

All these people might take on different roles in different parts of the text, and one way of defining their roles is to relate them to other parts of the text, rather than looking within and relating them to myself. If you look at the other small chapter [chapter 35] they seem to have different roles than they do in the beginning. It is important to recognise all these three in the Tales as kin. Although they do change, as the three forces change, they remain kin.

End of Session

Seminar 2 - Chapters 3, 4 & 5 of Beelzebub's Tales to His Grandson (continued)

Facilitator: Bonnie Phillips

Facilitator: Okay before we begin to look at the chapters four and five Sophia and I have been talking and I thought since she did such a nice lead-in with chapter two in order to discuss chapter three we though we would finish a bit with chapter three about the Captain explaining: "I was still only a sweeper on the long-distance ships of that period. Yes, a long, long, time has passed by, everything has undergone change and is changed since then, only Our Lord AND Sovereign remains unchanged."

So he is introducing here the fact that things do change and for me it is significant that he started out as the sweeper and is now the Captain addressing Beelzebub and is explaining to him, in chapters four and five, the first chapter four being The Law of Falling. We first run into, in The Law of Falling, The System of St. Venoma which was a system which was in use a short time, but it was an improvement upon the system that Beelzebub used while he was in our Solar System. And then we then move on to chapter five which is The System of The Archangel Hariton which replaced the System of Saint Venoma.

So, let's start with The Law of Falling

Participant 1: I think this is, for me quite important this particular bit because it gives us a clue that a lot of this is autobiographical. You see it tells us it means of operation of the first type of space-ship developed by St. Venoma and based on The Law of falling which is an improvement on the older type of ship. Now if you look at page 51 you see that the year, keeping it very simple, the year 223 in Objective Time round about 1921 of our time, it tells us that, so the year 185 in Objective time means 1883 of our time and it was in 1883 that Gurdjieff left home and made his first use of hypnotism and made his first pilgrimage which was to Echmiadzin. He studied three months at the Sarmoun monastery [unclear] and developed the friendship of [unclear] Pogossian and Abraham Yelov. This corresponds to the first system of St. Venoma which was a better method of psychological development. In 1884 he crystallized his motivation question after the significant [unclear]. In 1885 he went, he goes to Constantinople and meets Ekim Bay where he studies [unclear].

So if you go to page 69 here we are told that the Angel Hariton developed a new and better system [in the laboratory] for space-ships 23 years later, that would correspond to our own 1906 what was Gurdjieff doing at that time? It is suggested that from 1905 - 07 he was in an indeterminate

Seminar 1 - Chapters 3, 4 & 5 of Beelzebub's Tales to His Grandson (cont)

Central Asian Sufi community settling in Tashkent, then the capital of Russian Turkestan. We have got dates that correspond quite positively. Then when you go to chapter 5 even though the propulsion system of Arch-Angel Hariton is the one used [unclear reference to St. Venoma and Chapter 3] it seems to me that these are Sufi methods of psychological development which include, the last one which being known as 'the rapid method' , that is the source of that. So that to my mind there is no doubt that it is autobiographical.

Q. What is the source of it?

Participant 1: Well you should read Raphael LeFort some people think it is [legend] but it is not, it actually exists. He was taught the 'rapid method' of development by Sheik [?] but didn't use it in the same way he learned it. [?] Rapid method [unclear] so that's the source.

Participant 2: I just wanted to add a caveat about using dates and numbers in Gurdjieff I think numbers and Numerology are very important in Gurdjieff and no-one would deny that. But dates are really problematic because..

Participant 1: These aren't problematic, they are established.

Participant 2: How are they established?

Participant 1: Well if you read the stuff…

Participant 2: And where did he get them from?

Participant 1: I can't answer that from memory.

Participant 2: I know where he got them from, he got them from Gurdjieff . And Gurdjieff just never really told it exactly straight as far as dates go. Those of you who were here when Paul Taylor gave his talk about the dates, and these are dates that are taken from *Life is Real* and Paul Taylor gave a very good talk in which he pointed out that if we looked at the historical facts that Gurdjieff reports in that book when he was in New York he talks about events that actually happened but all the dates were wrong. So he uses dating in a symbolic way and that is something to bear in mind because Gurdjieff was where he said he was, he did do these things but because of Paul Taylor's research he didn't do these things on the dates he said he did and there is a lot of use of symbolic dates in that so I could recommend that.. It is just very difficult to say when Gurdjieff uses a date that is the date on which when something actually happened. It really is. It is big snare and a delusion I think,

Participant 3: Reading [Raphael LeFort's book? unclear] it seems to me that he was just writing out *Meetings*.

Participant 2: He took the dates that he got from Gurdjieff s texts but Gurdjieff's texts are not chronologically accurate.

Participant 4: Does this mean that he didn't mean the symbology as Dr. Sharp has pointed them out to us? He could have still meant to convey this symbology to us. We don't know why the dates that Gurdjieff used in his, say in his talks for instance, are not accurate. We don't know. He might have done that on purpose to get out a numerical 0 to us. We don't know.

Facilitator: But we are reminded here, by Objective Time calculation. What is it to be Objective about calculating time?

Participant 5: Well I think this is crucial actually. There are at least three time systems mentioned. There is this the Objective Time calculation which marked the, - reasonably considered to be zillions of years past the numbers, you know, whatever system you like to use since the creation of the world. Then there is the time on the planet Karatas which, at a conservative estimate is 389 times that of the planet Earth. Then you have got Earth time. So I think its tricky to take the 223 or whatever it is and start doing numerology on that in relation to Earth time. I question that.

Participant 6: I wonder if we could just agree to get back to the primary concern here in these chapters is the nature of the three space drives. At the 'speak, this is the captain speaking:

Q. "In our youth all such ships both for intersystem and for interplanetary communication [interesting that this is communication] were still run on the cosmic substance 'Elekilpomagtistzen,' which is a totality consisting of two separate parts of the omnipresent Okidanokh. And it was to obtain this totality that just those numerous materials were necessary which the former ships had to carry." [A&E p65]

That characterizes the first space-drive. Rather, how are we to understand the 'Elekilpomagtistzen' and so forth. But at least it gives us a starting-point to compare with the second space-drive and then compare with the third space-drive.

Prof. Thring: I would like to suggest that you also compare it with the way of the Fakir, the way of the Monk and the way of the Yogi and the Fourth way, because I think this is what it is all about.

Facilitator: Do you want to elaborate on that for us?

Prof. Thring: Well I must say the story about the Angel Hariton, the last one, fascinating. The way in which it is. [A&E p71]

Q. Where there is no resistance, contemporary ships like ours simply fall towards the nearest 'stability'; but in spaces where there are any cosmic substances which offer resistance, these substances, whatever their density, with the aid of this cylinder enable the ship to move in any, desired direction." Now I connect that with aphorism number three, which is the one about the

Seminar 1 - Chapters 3, 4 & 5 of Beelzebub's Tales to His Grandson (cont)

parts of your life where you have the greatest difficulty are the ones where you will be glad at the end of your life, you see. It is a tremendously important thing.

Facilitator: It was said earlier that these gases could represent thoughts or great difficulties and this ship makes better use of those difficulties.

Participant 7: The difficulties are the very things where the most emotional energy is available if we could only use it for the right thing instead of pouring it down the drain.

Participant 5: Could our Greek neighbor here tell us what Hariton means?

Participant 8: Hariton, I don't know the name in Greek because it is an old word. Hariton is from the Greek word Haris which means grace.

Participant 7: Yes. James George puts the same.

Participant 5: Yes say it nicely because it means grace.

Participant 8: Grace. The Holy Grace. Haris.

Participant 2: Well done; Grace!

Participant 5: Haris, Hariton.

Participant 6: It tells you a secret.

Participant 9: If; the second ship is it, which only had two aspects Okidanokh, that is, the third aspect is missing, because clearly, because of that [being] missing the quality on that ship, it was very cumbersome and difficult to steer etc. etc. But in the third ship he devises a cylinder with certain other qualities to it and one of those qualities is Amber, and amber is a symbol for impartiality. So impartiality is the key for me to this whole book, that impartiality was not in these other systems and Impartiality gives me the opportunity to move in any direction at all that I want to.

[unclear comment]

Everything is right in the title. It is an Objectively Impartial Criticism of the Life of Man and Objectivity and Impartiality are the two key words of the entire system and without that we know nothing. Everything else is interpretation and speculation but if I have the qualities of Impartiality and Objectivity then I have already arrived at a certain state which is much higher that the state I am [in] now. But we don't really understand what an experience of a state of Objectivity and Impartiality are.

Facilitator: No we don't and in the book he refers to our understanding of impartiality as only being part of what.

Participant 9: Because if I work upon myself my objective is to establish an objective intellectual center where my feelings are no longer feelings [in the sense we use them now] that become impartial and they become free of time because objectivity in the Gurdjieffian sense means there is an absence of associative thoughts and impartiality means the absence of associative feeling. So that's the whole key for me in chapter five that now we have an introduction of impartiality which gives me a much better vehicle on which to work from. If I understand from experience impartiality. And Impartiality does not belong on this earth and neither does Objectivity because we live in Subjectivity most of the time.

Comment: That is right.

Facilitator: Does anyone else have comments about the other materials used? We have spoken about the amber but how about the ivory and the platinum and what that might signify. It is a question which I have had.

Participant 9: And incidentally, I think, when in Egypt he described the Sphinx. The Sphinx has a ring of Amber around separating its head from its body and that is the ring of impartiality.

Comment: That is the Akhaldan symbol.

Participant 6: However we understand the three space-drives, to be consistent it seems we have to keep in mind that throughout the entire time of Beelzebub's isolation, exile in this system the inference is that it is all the first space-drive. He come here on the space-ship and then that space-ship is left to his supervision he can use that space ship for travel within that solar system. So however we understand the three space-drives to me it seems essential to have in mind that throughout the exile he is making use of the first space-drive.

Participant 7: Also there the bit of the cylinder that alternately opens and shuts

Participant 6: There is also some wacky science here too

Participant 7: If you take it literally, of course. Its not very practical engineering.

Participant 3: I mean that's how a four-stroke works, isn't it. It opens and shuts

Participant 7: In a way, yes. That would be like a V1.

Facilitator: Is that how we work? How we breathe?

Participant 5: Where is your platinum?

Seminar 1 - Chapters 3, 4 & 5 of Beelzebub's Tales to His Grandson (cont)

Facilitator: Oh, I don't know.

Participant 4: On page 75 of course there is of course the copper, anthracite and iodine.

Participant 5: That's the one.

Participant 2: It is the next chapter. Nick mentioned something about paying attention to the title and that is a really good old fashioned way of studying things, very practical. I just think there is in The Law of Falling, we have The cause of Delay and then we have The Law of Falling and a lot of themes about time are picked up. There are a lot of different references to time in different ways, the time in connection with these materials and the different times Chris mentioned. The Fall is about the creation of time. The story of The Fall is the creation of time. And I think there are many references we can pick up because fortunately I now know about the Archangel Hariton. I mean Saint Venoma has a very biblical ring to me, Saint Venoma? because he reminds me of the serpent of The Fall, of the poison. Whereas if the other angel is Grace then that gives you different. But they come within a kind o~ they are all references from within the Fall myth and the whole of the book is also a fall myth, it is about Beelzebub's fall and redemption. So the fact that he keeps on mentioning fall, fall, fall, presumably he is directing us to think about fall and the nature of time.

Participant 5: It is interesting that Saint Venoma's system just blasted the obstacles with blasts of 'Elekilpomagtistzen' which is hopefully a radical solution.

Participant 2: I think when you are talking about time it is important to recognize that are in certain states there is no time. Time and space are the [?] of the so called material universe.

Facilitator: Do you have a comment?

Participant 10: Yes It has been represented to me that the three space-ships represent the three sides of our development of personality. In the moving centre we move by pure force internally generated. The intellectual centre is drawn by things that are outside it. But the higher mental centre by the use of Impartiality can control what it is drawn by and moves thereby much more efficiently. And the three things that create those centres are the instinctive centre, the emotional centre and the higher emotional centre, the higher emotional centre corresponding to grace, the emotional centre corresponding to the Saintly Venoma. I think there is some pattern there anyway.

Participant 9: I think the 'open and shut' is to do with a similar analogy to Schrödinger's Cat. This cat, you don't know if its alive or dead until you open the box and then there is a collapse of an actuality wave..?]

Participant 7: That's a poor interpretation I don't agree with it. Schrödinger's interpretation is that the cat dies as the thing goes off whether you have observed it or not doesn't affect the situation. The paradox of the Fall interpretation is that clearly there is a period when the cat is both alive and dead which is nonsense. What happens in my view is quite simple that the quantum scale of things which is the disintegration the nucleus is subject to Plank's Constant therefore it is subject to Probability Laws. The moment it interacts with large scale things it ceases to be subject to Probability Laws and becomes an event. And at that moment is the moment when the disintegration upsets the [?]. Not the moment when the observer looks at it afterwards and if the observer had a window which was open all the time the result would be exactly the same. Therefore the poor interpretation, in my view, simply doesn't make sense.

Facilitator: We are about half-way through our discussion time.

Participant 6: Each of the three space-drives is a way of getting from here to there. In other words, when we are realizing an aim perhaps or the process of going from here to there. Beelzebub is exiled but there is a specific point, he is exiled to the planet Mars in this particular solar system. With the second space-drive there is the inference that one can realize an aim in terms of communication. This is after all communication that he is talking about here, inter-space, intersystem communication. And the third space-drive is the most efficient but it seems essential to keep in mind that one can go by any of the three. Beelzebub himself goes by the first space-drive when he is exiled and then throughout his exile on this solar system. The second space-drive is a kind of in-between sort of thing and there is finally the third space-drive. Trying to be Objectively Impartial it seems to me Gurdjieff has set out here something where here are improvements but you can still get there by any of these space-drives and there is some quality in there that I think it is important not to forget.

Participant 7: So you can by being what one would call a Fakir but it is a very slow process but you can get there.

Facilitator: What did you say Professor Thring?

Participant 7: I said that the Monk or the Fakir get there, or even if they don't in the end, they are much slower processes than the Fourth Way and that to me is the meaning of all this.

Participant 1: Some of us suggest that the little flap-valve is symbolic of the need to be open to new ideas and that the fuel used is anything, any situation one found oneself in so life itself and its events were the means of work upon oneself and which is what Gurdjieff emphasized the need to do the work now in life and not in a monastery etc.

Participant 9: When he talks about the ship which was designed to have windows that can open and shut that suggests to me that a window is transparent so in order to achieve any kind of objectivity or impartiality in whatever is observing me then I must become transparent to it. That is has something to look at and when I shut down my thoughts and feelings then that is too dense a situation for anything to observe me impartially and objectively because I am not open. So by being transparent it can see everything about me and that is the system.

Seminar 1 - Chapters 3, 4 & 5 of Beelzebub's Tales to His Grandson (cont)

Participant 11: [unclear reference to amber and electricity]

Participant 7: because amber is a very good electrical insulator it was able to produce these electrons when you rubbed it.

Participant 6: Now we come back to the anthracite, copper and the ivory. If you look at the electrical properties of these three, if you take anthracite and you burn it this is coal it is perhaps symbolically or 0 raising this question about things that are old and ancient and once had life and now have gone through a certain process etc. etc. perhaps. But its certainly as a reference to anthracite as coal it can produce heat through burning [comment it becomes volatilized] but it is lousy conductor of electricity. Copper is a very much better conductor of electricity but if you put a lot of current through it the copper gets very hot relative to the anthracite. When it comes to the ivory, ivory's distinguishing property is that ivory is an extraordinarily good electrical conductor. So maybe that setting them up that way then having them separated that there is something in each of the foods which if taken impartially will provide qualitatively certain levels of energy for what goes on inside us. At one level appropriately anthracite, at another level copper and on another level ivory. It is also interesting that copper is a naturally occurring mineral anthracite is coal made from previous life that has gone through a compression process of over hundreds of thousands, millions of years and ivory is a high representation, in the Eastern world, ivory was taken as Gurdjieff makes use of it also as one of the highest symbolic expressions of the spiritual- So perhaps all those things have something to do with this.

Participant 12: We are talking about energies and The Law of Falling can be seen more simply as gravity which may be opposed in our universe, the question of the movings of the cosmic bodies and having to do with gravity and what is holding the universe together but also expanding, we don't really know. We are talking about the 0 of matter. So much of this book is about the - the next chapter is called Perpetual Motion and historically about that time, that is in the early part of the twentieth century there was a lot of this business about people trying to create perpetual motion machines, but the book itself is about the changing of the stopinders so that the universe wouldn't collapse that our own part in that would not collapse, that there would continue to be the continual, transformation of energy so I see these things as all connected and having to do with energy transformation.

Participant 13: There is a point about energy transformation it is that a living being [as Schrödinger pointed out] has some mechanism for taking in a material of low entropy we will call it food and using it to create something of a very low entropy a highly ordered structure and throwing out the high energy waste products and as long as its alive it keeps on that process. And so this is the whole point about life is that a living being has this ability to maintain order in itself against the running down of time which is exactly what our universe has to do.

Participant 2: I wanted to say just as there was a correspondence between the last chapter we looked at and chapter 35 there is also a correspondence between this chapter and chapter 18. That is the chapter where Beelzebub goes to Saturn and he goes to Gornahoor Harharkh experimental place and if you look at it you will see a lot of similar references to glass-like structures and so on and this also had electricity and the passing of electricity in various directions. So it just says the other chapters are worth looking at together.

Participant 7: If you are going to have that then you have got to take the one where Gornahoor Harharkh [?]. It is literally true that electricity is one of the things that is destroying our society.

Participant 1: [unclear]

Participant 6: There is an inference here too that this is a digestive process. Whatever is out there is taken into the cylinder whenever the copper cylinder is opened and the force, the thrust comes from expansion. Expansion of what? Taking apart and digesting whatever it is that comes in and there are three levels inferred by what is coming in. Those three levels would be represented by the activity of the anthracite, the copper and the ivory. Whatever potential may exist in an event, perhaps the intellectual, emotional and physical sense, that whatever potential exists there, if that is expanded impartially inside of us then this becomes the third space-drive. This becomes the way in which we are projected or stay on track with our aim becomes a perpetual motion machine.
Because it can take in any event, any event, we will always have these three aspects that can interact at this interface and be digested so whatever comes from the anthracite which joins whatever comes from the copper and the ivory and this great expansion becomes how we go in whatever direction we wish to go in.

Participant 1: You can relate that to the digestion of food taking the first being food and in order for it to be brought to a higher energy level it has to be acted on by digestive enzymes already present which are at a higher level. In other words to make gold you have to have some gold.

Facilitator: Has there been enough discussion about The Law of Falling and this gravitational force and the use that is made of it or are there any other comments about that?

Participant 2: I don't want to say too much, it is just that The Fall is about descent and the creation of time and it is usually thought of a destructive, if you like. Whereas the Fall that Gurdjieff represents is positive and Bonnie began by mentioning that the Captain has evolved from being the sweeper and the ships evolved and they are connected with The Law of Falling and somehow it is a reversal of normal thinking about a fall and I think we ought to take that into account.

Participant 4: We don't always take things as they appear.

Participant 14: I see this expansion takes us out of this galaxy into more because it is movement.

Participant 7: It is also a part of modern cosmology that because of the law of gravity a temperature that is reached in certain stars which is sufficient to create the elements, so gravity, actually falling, does play a major role in the evolution of the whole universe. It creates the temperature inside stars which is sufficiently high to for the protons and neutrons to combine into

Seminar 1 - Chapters 3, 4 & 5 of Beelzebub's Tales to His Grandson (cont)

the higher elements. So we would never have any form other than the original protons and neutrons if it wasn't for gravity creating this tremendous energy inside stars.

Participant 1: That is what I think of as the Third Divine Emanation. [unclear] [tape change]

Participant 15: If it all happens by virtue of the Law of Falling how do you 'fall up' from the bottom of the enneagram process.

Participant 9: Because you have a system. Now you have a system because you know why you are going to do that. Because if I am beginning to try and work on myself I must have to create something which is going to scrutinize every single aspect of my life but I do that with the qualities of impartiality and objectivity because then I get the truth about myself which is absolute 'and no more hokey pokey about it..' And once I know the truth about myself and simultaneously I am beginning to grow because now I accept the truth about myself and from there I can grow. But if I only want to select certain aspects of my behavior then that is only partial so whatever it is I create to inspect me or whatever it is that accepts me for whatever I am accepts every bit of me whatever I am. So I have to go down to the very depths of where I am but with intelligence because I know why I am doing it and from there I can begin to [unclear].

Facilitator: In chapter four it is the first mention of Purgatory, talking about deaths. Purgatory carries with it all sorts of weighty notions about it.

Participant 4: Well to me it is the hardest chapter in the book. [unclear]

Participant 15: So what does that mean? On the way back up you come under the law of catching up?

Participant 4: You have to make a huge effort but it is based on knowledge.

Participant 9: It is like railway lines running parallel because I have got this ordinary life which I am now inspecting because now I have got this system to do that and running along parallel to that is an inner life which is growing all at the same time because it is running parallel and as I look along the horizon they eventually meet and join together.

Participant 8: We could talk about humility. [unclear]

Participant 14: The falling becomes centrifugal force. [unclear] It is not a simple fall at all

Participant 7: It is very interesting because this earth is freely falling towards the sun. It is falling under the acceleration towards the sun only it happens to have a velocity round so a it goes in that direction.

Participant 6: But not only the Sun falls to the bottom and that is what he says. Wherever you happen to be it is the concentration that we fall towards whether it is the planet or the Sun or whatever.

Facilitator: Or whether its ourselves.

Participant 6: One of the things which we haven't mentioned yet that is in the circumstance of the second space drive of St. Venoma, remember how difficult it is for the people who are responsible for running the space-ship. They have to slow down, and the qualifications of this system are really important they have to slow down and they have to make a great many calculations and they do all of this, especially the calculation, not from themselves. They are trained, have been trained beforehand by very high individuals, beforehand. They simply are doing what they are told. You do it this way. You make this calculation under these circumstances and you have to slow the whole process down in order to be able to finally take aim and shoot.. I mean when you pull aside the screening and so forth. So he makes it a, he describes it, this is a very difficult, tedious process that has no individuality. There is no individual 'decisioning' going on in this. The decisions are made around a formula or a recipe, if you will, that has been directed from above. All the people running the space-ship are trained and they do exactly how they are trained so however we understand the second space-drive we have got to include that in it.

Participant 2: I must hurry on. I don't think it is clear, I mean actually within the text what happens when you get to the planet, it says that they fall to the nearest concentration but it doesn't say how, it says that it moves in empty space quite easily but it doesn't say how it leaves the atmosphere of the planet, it just doesn't explain that. .I mean I know you can relate it to work ideas or to oneself but actually in the text it is a problem and I think it is important to look at omissions in Gurdjieff's texts where he doesn't explain it to you and look at what isn't said as well because there lots of places where what he says is anomalous. One which is a of that is where the rotations of the Moon and the crops, which I won't go into now because its too late in the day and I don't think I could manage it, but its absurd it doesn't work out, and this was pointed out me by a very famous astronomer who is good on rotations and he actually wrote me a piece about it. So in fact it is not the case that everything makes sense.

Participant 4: Mister G never promises that it's easy to coat your being-body, to get back to His Endlessness. Look at those wonderful, struggling people, or souls in Purgatory [chapter] endeavoring to get back to His Endlessness. He never in any of his themes says that this going up or perfecting your being-bodies or Beelzebub arising again this is always he says it will be very difficult..

Facilitator: It must have been very difficult for the Captain who was a sweeper.

Participant 14: [unclear] [archangel Hariton?]

Seminar 1 - Chapters 3, 4 & 5 of Beelzebub's Tales to His Grandson (cont)

Participant 12: Even Beelzebub only got to the third degree of reason before Endlessness which says to me that [with what you say] we can get close to being Endlessness but never completely Endlessness. That is how I see it.

Participant 3: [unclear - purgatory.]

Participant 16: We haven't read the chapter in the book.

Participant 12: You can go real close but it is just a feeling I get. You can't quite return to the source as long as there is a manifest appearance, something like that. Its not spelled out but you do [get a feel for it] and he does say 'up to the third degree'.

Participant 7: I always put all those things alongside a very odd paradox that Paradise and Hell are here beside us at the moment. That to me is very, very important.

Participant 17: What is the second degree?

Participant 7: Well the highest degree, there are three aren't there. The highest and then the one which is the highest that can be reached by three-brained-beings and of them and then the one that Beelzebub has reached. I have forgotten their names but they are all known by a name.

Facilitator: OK we are about the end of our time. Are there any other comments on chapters 4 and 5?

Participant 6: Only the difference, [unclear] The difference between the second space-drive is created by a Saint, the space drive is created by an Angel and the first space-drive is unattributed. Again it is one of these things we have to ponder.

Participant 7: One other point I'd like to make and that is people talk about the name Saint Venoma in terms of venom. But James George interpreted it as 'come to mother' [laughter]

Participant 12: There are so many things that we haven't dealt with, the wooly beings and so on.

Facilitator: There is so much more. Thank you everyone.

End of Session

Informal Recollections of Meetings with Gurdjieff and Ouspensky

Professor M. W. Thring

A Participant speaking: I was told that Professor Thring would like to hear something that I more or less accidentally took with me in my luggage. It is a small disc that contains some material that has never before been listened to by other people. We will hear three things - one a little story told by Gurdjieff that one is fairly well known, so you will hear his voice.

Prof. Thring: His voice?

A Participant: His voice. This story has been a [paper?] then you will hear two selections. These were quite recently made from old taped material relocated been, the tapes have been taken care for. They were in very bad condition and they have been put in a digital reel And so what you hear [in part] are two evenings in G's apartment in Paris in 1949. August 1949. You will hear him play his organ and occasionally say something to a child and so on. But it is very exciting because these have been relocated and actually you are the first group that ever hears this material The first lot is known a bit ... then you hear the organ and it is very soft very beautiful. Was I clear?

[Yes - from those assembled]

A Participant: It will take about 15 minutes or so.

Prof. Thring: I'll be delighted to hear it.

[The tape is played and listened to, followed by a short pause]

Prof. Thring: Thank you for that. That was absolutely wonderful. It brought it all back. You know, it had the same effect as when I heard it in Gurdjieff's flat [unclear]. I don't want to break with the feeling of this, it was so wonderful but I thought I might pass these round [3 wooden sculptures which were passed along for those present to hold and examine] so that everybody can have the pleasure of feeling them.

This is The Sphinx although as Mr. A. [actual names omitted] said. I have put a head on that and a tail. And this one is called The Perfected Human Being and the Hawk of Egoism and the Dove of conscience are the same size. All their legs are the same size; that would be Harmonious Development where everything is rightly balanced. Because the outer leg of the Hawk is 'make your way in the world' [as Gurdjieff said a man should be able to support 22 people [unclear] but the inner leg is self-perfection which is still Egoism. The outer leg of the Dove is 'love thy neighbor as thyself and the inner leg is 'seek for the purpose of the Universe and try to serve it'. And the harmonious person has all four legs the same size whereas our civilization... [unclear] This one is called 'as above so below' because it represents at the lowest level the methane atom CH_4 with the Carbon in the centre joined to four Hydrogen atoms by the valency bonds and then they are joined together by the Hydrogen bond. It has ten triads in it [unclear] and has of course five spheres all joined together so that none of the lines cross [unclear] yet every one is joined to the others [forming a poly-centred tetrahedron].

And on the human level, the Perfected Human, these three are the three centres of the planetary body. This is the Body Kesdjan or the Objective Conscience and this is Objective Reason or the soul in the notation of Beelzebub, of course there is the notation of Ouspensky also but it is the completed human being on that level on a higher level and on the highest level it is an old symbol for The Trinity.

What I want to say more than anything is that I worked with Ouspensky and Bennett for about twelve years if not thirteen, the end of '37 to '48, eleven years. Ouspensky died and actually in 1949 I happened to be in America and they immediately published, Mme Ouspensky published, *In Search of the Miraculous* which Ouspensky had refused to publish because of Gurdjieff's book. So I had ten copies of it to bring back and I came back on the Queen Elizabeth so I didn't have the weight of it on the plane. [unclear] The point was with Ouspensky, it was in effect philosophical knowledge we got really. You knew you had 'many I's, you knew that you couldn't DO and that you had to 'not express' negative emotions and so on and we worked on these things all those years. And we had all the diagrams that are in *In Search of the Miraculous* and there was quite a lot to go on, but somehow it was all hopeless. There was no hope there, you couldn't do [unclear] but when we went to Paris it was entirely different, it was like going into a different world, a world in which negative emotions and trivial things... they just weren't there. It was like a world in which you were free of all that. You were just concerned with the Work. We started doing the movements and I am hopeless at the movements because I am totally un-musical but I got enough of them to realise what kind of work, what kind of control of attention, complete control of attention in all the centres is necessary for that. So I got a taste for what that means. [unclear]. The most important thing I got from Paris was the idea of sensing your body, and also sitting quietly and sensing your limbs and so on. And even then I got the sense of opening oneself and freeing oneself from the thoughts that go on all the time and the associations in the moving centre and the associations in the intellectual centre, being free of these. So I got a taste of what it is all about. And I got hope, there was a message of hope, always. It wasn't 'cannot do' it was trying to do work. The impression I got of Mr. Gurdjieff was entirely different from the impression I had from Ouspensky and Bennett. It was the impression that I can only describe as Universal Benevolence. He really wanted you and me, everybody, to be influenced towards developing themselves as a result of being in contact with him and his emanations. This was very, very strong and it has been with me ever since. I don't think I want to describe particular events. We took our 6yr old daughter over at one point. And well, I will describe that. Mr. Gurdjieff cut an orange in half and ate it by pushing it out with his chins through the juice like this [illustrates]. And he said to Susan

All & Everything Conference 2001

'You eat it like that.' And she looked at Mr. Gurdjieff and said 'No I won't!' And she peeled and ate the orange in the ordinary way. Margaret was very upset you see but Mr. Gurdjieff simply said 'Not very suggestible' and of course it meant that he was admiring her.

One personal thing was that I always tried to drink the toasts honourably and you had to drink. The men had to drink a third of a medicine glass full of either vodka or Armagnac at every toast and we had sixteen toasts at the meal and it was far more alcohol that I had ever had in an evening before and I was sick in his inner sanctuary as a result of [unclear] which was very valuable experience because it destroyed at once one particular branch of my vanity I have never had since. [Laughs] It was quite an experience but it was really worthwhile. And another thing was that once I was bit befuddled before the toasts and I was sitting next to Mme De Salzmann and Mr. Gurdjieff spoke to her in Russian and I nodded! Because I was so drunk I thought I could understand it! And I really couldn't. But Mr: Gurdjieff of course immediately spotted it at once: 'You understand Russian?' 'No Sir!' Why you nod?' He was absolutely on the ball.

So, that is what I want to give you this evening. The emotional effect of going to the flat all those times that I did. That it has somehow been with me as the spurs of memory that I can feel, ever since.

If anybody wants to ask me questions about Gurdjieff I will try and answer.

Question: [unclear]

Answer: My impression of Mr. Gurdjieff was that he was, ... that he worked so much on himself and suffered so much, had been through so much that he was entirely on a different level. There was something sacred. A real messenger from above [God?] That is my personal opinion anyway.

Question: Can you tell us how you felt when you knew you were going to see him for the first time?

Answer: I was very excited. We got up at five o'clock in the morning and I drove my little old car across on the ferry and got to Paris by lunchtime. I thought well I shall be so excited that I shall stay awake in spite of having this long drive and getting up too early. But in fact I sat down cross-legged on the floor and somebody came in - oh - maybe it was [unclear] Bennett or someone and read a long chunk of Beelzebub and I fell asleep. [laughs] So the excitement wasn't there. But when he came in and we saw him this was priceless. You see we had always been told by Ouspensky that G had gone mad. We had heard that for years and years and years and suddenly to hear that he was alive and we could go to see him was marvellous.

Question: And how did that happen?

Answer: Because Mme Ouspensky, the moment Ouspensky died rang up Bennett and the people at Lyme Place and so on and said 'Go over to Mr. Gurdjieff at such and such an address' and so

Informal Recollections of Meetings with Gurdjieff and Ouspensky

they did. And Gurdjieff apparently said that he was delighted with Ouspensky. He said 'Now he is my friend' because he had seen ... [unclear] *In Search of the Miraculous*. It is marvellous we have got two different formulations of his teaching. Some of them disagree quite a lot. The Moon for example, in *In Search of the Miraculous* is the growing tip of creation in Beelzebub's Tales. It was an awful mistake. But they do together produce a very powerful effect, and its very important. That's what I am glad to do in my book is to put them together from both the references to things from both books and from all the others, from Views from The Real World and so on. It is so important that you don't just have one verbal formulation. You have different verbal formulations which apparently at first sight disagree and that's the way you get towards something real. I think we are incredibly fortunate to have had Mr. Gurdjieff

Question: When was it you actually saw him, what year?

Answer: It would have been June 1948.

Question: Over a year before he died.

Answer: Yes, and I did see him again. I saw him - I must have gone over there for long weekends about six or eight times altogether before Christmas when he went over to the States for Christmas that year. Then I saw him again in the spring.

Then I had a nervous breakdown in the summer and then I went to America with my [unclear] for two months in September and October and soon after I got back he died. He was planning to make another trip to America when he died. I expect he knew he was going to die. It was all part of this, you know, he would keep people moving and doing things and changed them because it was all part of his method.

Question: Did Mr. Gurdjieff work with you privately or was it in the group setting.

Answer: I'll have to answer that honourably. Once we had a toast and I had the last drink out of the bottle. And Bennett said to me, 'If you have the last drink out of the bottle you've got to bring a dozen bottles'. So I borrowed money from [unclear] and bought a dozen bottles of the cheapest Armagnac I could get. It was pretty late and I took them over, delivered them to the door.

Mr. Gurdjieff invited me in and sat me down in his study and said 'Now what have you got?' And he gave me the same task which is in Margaret Anderson's book and which I've been doing ever since. You can find it there. It is also in my book [unclear] but it is something which has meant something to me ever since.

Question: Did you have any experience with his teachings on meditation?

Answer: We were given the task by Mme De Salzmann of sitting quietly three times a day. Curiously enough [unclear reference to postures]

All & Everything Conference 2001

Question: Was that while Mr. Gurdjieff was alive? That you were given the meditation by Mme De Salzmann?

Answer: Yes, yes, it was during … on one of the visits to Paris.

Question: Was that something which was an active something you were doing with sensing the body or was it a receptive.

Answer: Probably both.

Question: It was both. Probably?

Answer: I don't think [unclear]

Comment: Yes.

Question: Was there anybody there who had acquired the same sort of power as Gurdjieff?

Answer: Oh yes of course. Mme De Salzmann.

Question: Did you do the movements? At the Salle Pleyel?

Answer: Yes, at the Salle Pleyel.

Question: Upstairs? Never on the ground [level]?

Answer: Never on the ground. I seem to remember having it upstairs. It was a long time ago.

Question: Who played [for] the movements?

Answer: Mme De Sal7rnann. There were also some French people who [unclear]

Question: [unclear] [Did Mr. Gurdjieff direct these?]

Answer: No, but he would come and watch.

Question: Can you remember who each of you were. Their names and so on? Answer: I made a list of them. I gave them to Mrs. Courtney-Mayers.

Question: [unclear] [Regarding the rooms at G's Paris flat]

Answer: I don't remember.

Comment: Yes he does, [here a section of tape is inaudible] ... One gets the impression as Prof. Thring will know that the flat was absolutely chock-a-block with painting and knickknacks and cabinets of eggs and all that. It is an absolute paradise, it is like an Aladdin's Cave. You go in there and all your childish feelings of joy and bliss are aroused by this sort of fantasy richness of the whole place. So it doesn't actually tend to pay to go into that much technical interest in the place, wouldn't you say?

Prof. Thring: Yes, I would agree. There was also usually the smell of cooking.

Comment: Well that wasn't there when I was there.

Prof. Thring: Certainly a lot of the paintings were absolute daubs that he had bought from Russian refugees. And there were these cabinets full of these Chinese, or china dolls.

Question: [unclear]

Answer: I honestly don't remember it is 51 years ago and I wasn't in much of a mood for studying my surroundings. I was concerned with the atmosphere. I mean there was an emanation which you could feel, and it affected you.

The first time I went of course, was only a week after Gurdjieff's second car crash.

And he was terribly weak, he couldn't eat anything, he was absolutely blue and yet he insisted on having the toasts and everything going through. And you could see that he was making enormous efforts that he was holding himself alive for this last period in which he was trying to bring together all the groups that had started Work. That is my strongest impression. He held himself alive, I mean he told us that he was going to live two hundred years and I believed him! [laughter] But that was one of his... I mean he knew he was dying. But he was holding himself alive against great pain in order to bring together the groups from various countries - the French, The English, The Americans and some of the others. .. and try and get them together round the table: Although the French rather suffered when the English were there, because they couldn't get a table and had to form a chain into the kitchen.

Question: With respect to Ouspensky. Could you say anything about what you perceived as his feeling about Mr. Gurdjieff? That is, did he, was he, I mean, happy because G didn't welcome him? Or did he welcome him back or was it a situation where he didn't want any part of Gurdjieff?

Answer: I think that he had, as has been said in James Moore's book that he had twice taken away Ouspensky's groups that had built up and he jolly well wasn't going to let him do it again. [tape change]

Question: [unclear] the last days of Ouspensky described as highly dramatic states [unclear]

Answer: I heard about it but I didn't witness it. You see, the first time I went to America was in '49 when he was already dead. I was in America in'49 from September till October.

Question: Somebody told me that at the last meeting a few weeks before Ouspensky died he, Ouspensky had said, 'I have abandoned the method, it does not give the required results. Is that right? [unclear]

Answer: I don't know. All I know is that I didn't get the feeling from Ouspensky that there was a way through and I did get it from Gurdjieff

Question: [unclear]

Answer: I was present at the meeting at Colet Court or whatever its called[Gardens] when all Ouspensky's pupils were there and he said that he was going to go to America, that Europe was finished because these two men, wild beasts Hitler and Stalin were going to smash us.

Question: Were going to what? I'm sorry, they were going to smash us.

Answer: They were going to smash Europe and England and he was going to America Question: Were you a witness to the parting of the ways between Mr. Ouspensky and Mr. B?

Answer: One of them; because it happened twice: Ouspensky actually said to me that Bennett was panicking [man].

Question: That was the first or the second one?

Answer: This was the first. Bennett got terrified because there were trouble[s] with his work duties and groups and he disconnected from 4uspensky: The final time [unclear] But I went on with Bennett of course because Ouspensky was away in America.

Question: Did you attend Mr. Gurdjieff's funeral?

Answer: No I didn't. I had just comeback from America and I had to attend to my job. I couldn't get away: My sister Bryn saw Gurdjieff in the American hospital but I don't think she stayed for the funeral she wrote to my wife about it, how she had a great experience seeing his body in the morgue.

Question: How about Ouspensky? Were you there? Were you able to say goodbye to him when he died?

Answer: No, no. He came back to England and then was driven round but I only heard about it afterwards.

Informal Recollections of Meetings with Gurdjieff and Ouspensky

Question: Then how many more years did you stay with Mr. Bennett?

Answer: I really kept myself away from Bennett after my nervous breakdown in '49.

Question: Can you explain why most, many people in Gurdjieff groups link Gurdjieff and Ouspensky together as if they were equals when it is more like a Mozart and Salieri situation? I can never understand that.

Answer: I wouldn't try to explain it either. I think its an interesting analogy. [unclear]

Comment: But there is a good reason for it in a sense that because of the publication of Fragments so a lot of people got to know the Work through Ouspensky and they saw Ouspensky as being the same as Gurdjieff. I think that in my experience that is how I have met people who have come across Work and after all he was around much more, and is read much more than *Beelzebub's Tales* and eventually the others too. I would hazard a guess that has something to do with it.

Comment: It's easier language.

Prof. Thring: Its much, much easier to understand and to take hold of *In Search of the Miraculous*. Its bound to be [unclear]

Comment: Its more popular.

Question: Can you tell me about when you first heard readings or had any copies to read of *Beelzebub's Tales*. Did you have these before? Did you have these before you went to Paris to meet Mr. Gurdjieff?

Answer: No, no, no, no, no. We went to Paris in '48 and this book was published in '51. We did, my wife and I contributed £100 [One hundred Pounds]to the publication. We were told that it needed money for publication. In fact I've got the letter about it needing money which is [I have a copy of it here, this passed around] interesting. And so did my sister, Bryn, so I have now the copy which we got which is copy 183 and she has, I think 184 which I've got because she is dead and I took it.

Question: Can you speak about your first impression of the book?

Answer: Well we had pieces of it read when we went to sit at the meals, that is before lunch and before supper. We had pieces of the first, second even third series read to us. So we had, and he always, Gurdjieff specially selected the piece of *Beelzebub* that we had, or that he thought was just right for us at that point. And of course it was difficult listening to it.

Question: Were any of the readings that you heard of the chapter The Holy Planet Purgatory?

All & Everything Conference 2001

Answer: Good question and I don't know the answer I don't remember on that point, no.
But I do know that of course the Holy Planet Purgatory was that he used to asked people to read especially and its quite likely that it was but I just don't remember. What interests me the HPP and the earlier one The Arch-Absurd covers the same question about the creation of the universe in slightly different terms but still not fitting together. [pause] And, I think the point about this, you see. Ouspensky was a journalist and he could write quite well and clearly and be easy to understand from that point of view. Gurdjieff deliberately made his book very difficult, sentences a whole page long so that you've got to puzzle over it. You've got to be persistent with it.

Question: Do you think, I mean I don't know if you have an opinion but the hopelessness that you say Ouspensky, that there was no hope, you couldn't do anything, this is very strong in Fragments and he reports it as coming from Gurdjieff. I just wondered do think this feeling of hopelessness is coming from Ouspensky all the time, or, do you feel Gurdjieff s teaching changed a great deal from the beginning?

Answer: I don't think it changed, no. I think it was Ouspensky's caste of character that [unclear] in that book. I don't believe Gurdjieff ever taught that it is hopeless.

Comment: And yet Gurdjieff was pleased with Fragments, wasn't he?

Answer: Oh yes, because Fragments is a very clear account of the theory so to speak - beautifully written and it adds a lot to the knowledge and I think that Bb contains far more if you can get down to it. Far more, in fact when he, in the Second Series he keeps promising to put a whole lot of things in the Third Series it is my view that they are in here, hidden away deeply. For all those things he says he will write about he has written about and they are hidden away.

Question: Do you think he gave, animated a feeling of hope when he was in Russia that's what I want to... Do you think he had that feeling then.

Answer: I'm sure he had because the message he came back from was; there is a way! That was his message. There is a way and I think I am going to try and communicate it to you. You see this is where religions fall down in my opinion, they don't tell you a way.

Comment: I might just come in here to say, if you read the story of Ouspensky in Finland and one or two other episodes like that, the reason why he didn't stay with him you can also track through J G Bennett's witness and things like that you get the impression that Mr. Ouspensky was desperate for a system, that was his whole character and way of operating. Gurdjieff was really interested in a way of being. [unclear]

Although Ouspensky reports the teaching about Knowledge and Being etc. he was still interested in the system and I think it is the emotional physical axis of the Gurdjieff work that somehow he patently couldn't handle. If I may say so. And this is very, very interestingly characteristic of the fact that a great many of the what I would call less valid, more spurious, more systematic, more dogmatic groups all come from and quote heavily from Fragments and Ouspensky and its very different from some of the groups that have struggled to remain open to this different dimension that [Prof. Thring] has been in. I think that if you really study it objectively it is very striking that [there is] this shift by the Ouspensky mind in a certain direction.

Comment: He does say at the end of In Search that he saw it developing into a religion and that's why he abstained from it [unclear].

Comment: I can't remember when but at the last stages of Ouspensky he does say quite clearly that there is no system and that links in with what you are saying.
[unclear section]

Question: What about *The Psychology of Man's Possible Evolution*? [unclear]

Answer: I haven't used it in my [unclear] although I have read it. It was very much the same thing as he gave in his introductory lectures that I went to.

Question: So each time that you went did Gurdjieff play his own music on the organ?

Answer: Not always, no. It was a great privilege when he would come last thing at night at about one o'clock in the morning, and we had finished the meal and he would say 'Come into the other room, sit a little '[unclear] and we would sit down and he would play his organ.

And it was wonderful; it brought it all back to me. You see I am totally un-musical and yet I was always moved, deeply so [unclear] it was there.. and that same power was moving me.

Comment: I am sure we are all pleased [unclear] Yes, it was, it was wonderful Comment [unclear]

Prof. Thring: Gurdjieff had a great sense of humour and made wonderful jokes. It created part of the atmosphere, yes. Often jokes. One thing I do remember and I'll perhaps mention. One day the postman came with some parcel to deliver. Gurdjieff invited him in, sat him down with us and gave him a glass of Armagnac, you see, and the postman drank it, said thank you and went out. And Gurdjieff beamed at us, you could see he felt that postman had being, you see, he had made contact with that person. It was the same when he gave sweets to children I'm sure he made some contact with them.

Question: Did you ever experience Mr. Ouspensky in that way? I mean I never read about him having any relationship with children or...

Question: [unclear - cats?]

Answer: I don't think he did, no. He would ride round on his horse when we were working at Lyme Place. I did a lot of work on the roof of the boathouse there. also [unclear] they had to install a huge great gas-engine to make the electricity. No, that's right they had a huge great gas engine before with an enormous flywheel. Then there was a danger of not having any gas. So we installed a gas-producer which would run on anthracite to make gas to run the, no not run the big gas engine but to run the small car engine run on gas to make the electricity. There were some quite good engineers so I was usually in the engineering team.

Question: Why do you laugh? [asks someone, who replies] Because you were an engineer?

Prof. Thring: Yes. Oh dear [unclear - not?] that I was a good engineer. It was a chap named Mills who was a good engineer.

Question: How was Bennett with children?

Answer: I think it was more theoretical than loving. That is my impression. I mean my children were up then [unclear] but they were always a bit of a nuisance at Coombe Springs [unclear] And I'm sorry to say that my two elder children, the ones who used to go there have resisted any kind of spiritual development. The younger one who was born in 1949 is more open than the other ones who were put off by the single-minded attitude at Coombe Springs. [pause] I think what [a person present] said is very important. [addressing him] I think what you said is very important. I was very glad you said it.

Question: About?

Answer: About the people who worked as a result of Ouspensky and the people who worked as a result of Gurdjieff

Comment: That's the way I feel about it.

Prof. Thring: I would agree with it.

Question: What did you say?

Comment: Well I've said it, I mean, a whole long speech. [unclear]

Prof. Thring: [laughs.]

Comment: Oh, I don't want anybody to listen to me. I want everybody to please evaluate for yourselves, really well, how it reads in Fragments about the way that Ouspensky kind of distances himself from Gurdjieff, and the number of re-entries he was offered at the Prieure etc. etc. And how it was that he wouldn't let, wouldn't read *Beelzebub*, wouldn't let people look at it and said Gurdjieff was mad etc. etc. And the kind of influence that the two people [fighting] seemed to exert on those groups and circles. And I must say here that I'm very happy to be [unclear] ... a kind of, em, black and white spirit that book has as distinct from the incredibly rich texture that we have in *Beelzebub's* and in *Views* and in all of Gurdjieff's writings. There is this sense of richness and struggle and the fact that you read the first Series, he was still working right up to the end, I'm sure, right up to the end, when you say when he had his injuries he was still...

Prof. Thring: And that one could feel that he had really paid the price.

Comment: That's not to belittle the value of *Fragments* as a primer in terms of the ideas at a certain stage of their evolution and presentation. That's not to belittle that book I would give it to any first student in order to gradually wean them on the [unclear]

Prof. Thring: That is why I have deliberately compared the two in my book. The way the difference I find is that Gurdjieff - the two things, for example the word 'conscience' is dealt with in both books because I think adding the two together makes four!

Comment: Absolutely.

Comment: The difference I find is that the Gurdjieff group which is really Ouspensky [unclear] is primarily concerned with Remembering Oneself as an exercise. And the group, the beginners, would go round one by one and talk about experiences which they had in remembering themselves or forgetting themselves. One guy says that he made, a sign for himself saying Remember Yourself but he kept forgetting to look at it.

Prof. Thring: If I may say so this is very interesting because under Ouspensky it was "Remember Yourself" but when we got to Paris it was "Do I Am." This is a fact!

Comment: That is so interesting because if you ask somebody from the Ouspensky stream, "What do you do to remember yourself", you really get the biggest load of spaghetti you can imagine. But if you ask a [unclear] student, even quite a young person who has been through the very traditional sort of Gurdjieff pupil group they will be much more related to this sense of returning to the cognizance of your own organic reality as a basis from which it is possible to [exceed?] thought, feeling [unclear] and isn't that a very different perspective and certainly much more practical [unclear] so thank you for drawing attention to that difference, very strong, very strong.

Prof. Thring: It was [unclear] but very striking. Because people would say, well what is Self Remembering? You know.

Comment: You can still ask that "You what is Self Remembering?"

Question: You said earlier that some of the readings that you heard were from the Third Series, in the apartment?

Answer: I think so, yes, I have that impression.

All & Everything Conference 2001

Question: Do you have any impression about whether he intended to complete the book [unclear].

Prof. Thring : My feeling is that book is in fact complete and that was what he had meant to do and all the things he promised in the Second series he will do in the Third Series are packed into here [indicates First Series] hidden away! Its all there, and the Third Series he never intended to write a huge great tome for it. That's my personal opinion. But if you read the Third Series properly it contains an enormous amount of direct psychological advice. I mean if you are reading the Third Series by itself will really give you a way of become something. He gives tasks in it. He explains things.

Question: [unclear]

Prof. Thring: In the Third Series he does explain how you have to have a sensation of taking air into yourself then as you breathe out something spreads through your whole body. That's in the Third Series. Now that's...

Comment: [unclear]

Question: During the readings of All & Everything and the different books did students ask questions.

Answer: We didn't ask questions, no.

MB: Professor Thring, we want to thank you very much. We certainly don't want to keep you here all night and we probably would. Thank you.

[applause]

To Destroy Mercilessly...

Keith A. Buzzell

When Gurdjieff set out to create a 'written legominism' he was well aware of the extraordinary difficulties he was to encounter. In part, the opening chapter of the Three Series, "The Arousing of Thought" is a testament to his recognition of these difficulties, at the same time containing both indications and examples of how he was to undertake the resolution of those difficulties. While written language has been rightly pointed to as one of man's crowning achievements in communication it has also been identified as a primary source of confusion, contradiction, disagreement and the furtherance of ignorance rather than truth.

Gurdjieff captures the essence of this quandary in his differentiation of "mentation by thought" and "mentation by form"[1] this in the context of discussing what a "conscious thinker" should be aware of:

"Man has in general two kinds of mentation, mentation by thought, in which words, always possessing a relative sense, are employed; and the other kind, which is proper to all animals as well as to man, which I would call "mentation by form".

The second kind of mentation, that is, "mentation by form", by which, strictly speaking, the exact sense of all writing must be also perceived, and after conscious confrontation with information already possessed, be assimilated, is formed in people in dependence upon the conditions of geographical locality, climate, time, and, in general, upon the whole environment in which the arising of the given man has proceeded and in which his existence has flowed up to manhood.

Accordingly, in the brains of people of different races and conditions dwelling in different geographical localities, there are formed about one and the same thing or even idea, a number of quite independent forms, which during functioning, that is to say, association, evoke in their being some sensation or other which subjectively conditions a definite picturing, and which picturing is expressed by this, that, or the other word, that serves only for its outer subjective expression.

That is why each word, for the same thing or idea, almost always acquires for people of different geographical locality and race a very definite and entirely different so to say "inner content". "

---

[1] 'Arousing of Thought' pp 15-17, *Beelzebub's Tales to His Grandson*

The 'picturing' of a *whole* event, for which the word serves as a compression or "outer subjective expression", seems to be the key here. Gurdjieff is emphasizing that there is great hazard in the use of words. If the word reflects mentation by thought alone then it is *disconnected* from the other two brains - it cannot reflect the lawfulness that is imbedded in a whole (three brained) event. It is a *disembodied abstraction* that will inevitably be interpreted within a context that is provided by the *hearer* of the word - and he will "of course infallibly understand that same word in quite another sense".

The best way to avoid this 'abstraction pitfall' is to create a whole, three-brain image of an experience, one that will incorporate sensation, feeling and thought (as the "outer subjective expression"). In this way a triad, or lawful expression, can be taken in as impression by the listener (or reader) and a more whole and precise "inner content" can be communicated. Throughout *The Tales*, Gurdjieff makes use of this *simultaneity* of speaking to the three brains (the conscious and the subconscious), thereby providing appropriate data for confrontation that will comprise real food for digestion.

Gurdjieff creates many of these 'picturing', or three-brain images, by telling short stories (e.g. the Transcaucasian Kurd, the death of his grandmother), or longer, more elaborate stories (e.g. the Bokharian Dervish), but he also demonstrates the use of 'mentation by form' in his selection and combination of individual words.

It is his selection of individual words, and the "inner content" that is present in their etymology, that I would like to explore with you this morning. Hopefully this type of exploration will provide an experiential, three brain confirmation of the value of 'mentation by form'.

*   *   *

Our aim is to highlight a number of questions that arise from Gurdjieff's written intention concerning the First Series, *Beelzebub's Tales to His Grandson*.

On the Frontis page to the 1950 Edition Gurdjieff states that his intention is:

"To destroy, mercilessly, without any compromises whatsoever, in the mentation and feelings of the reader, the beliefs and views, by centuries rooted in him, about everything existing in the world."

On the opening page (1184) of 'From the Author' a somewhat different phrasing of his intention replaces 'destroy' with 'corrode'... The word 'destroy' is changed to 'extirpate' in the 1974 Edition, and in the 1992 version, the expression 'to sweep away' replaces 'corrode'.

Beelzebub's Tales is looked upon by people of Work as a source of truth. At the outset, however, he emphasizes that destruction of our views and beliefs is his overriding intent. Clearly, 'our'

To Destroy Mercilessly… - Questions & Answers

Facilitator: On our visit to Two Rivers Farm last fall, we set this question of 'Destroy' in front of a general group of approximately 45-50 people and it turned into a very useful and interesting discussion. Quite a number of folks were ready to admit that they had not entered into a discussion of this kind before. In other words, to ask this question such that we can reach a point where we can discover the nuances of meaning and Gurdjieff's intent in using the words "Destroy, Mercilessly". We have, by definition, corrosion, chemical disintegration, absolute destruction, rooting out, setting the dogs on etc. There are many potential ways of looking at this. It is a useful exploration to ask, how do we extirpate a belief or view? How do we do that? How do you get rid of them? Do you do it bit by bit? Do you tear out the roots? Do you take off the stem? Do you just cut it off? How do we approach these beliefs and views?

What we did at the farm was that we looked at these questions and began by sharing perspectives on what it meant to "destroy mercilessly the beliefs and views rooted by centuries about everything existing in the World."

So, how do *you* understand this process of destruction?

Participant 1: When I first read about "Destroying Mercilessly", I was quite ready to be rooted out, in fact I was looking for the ideas that would answer what I was looking for.

Facilitator: To replace?

Participant 1: Yes, to replace. The ideas found a ready home.

Facilitator: Why?

Participant 1: I was dissatisfied with my understanding.

Facilitator: So there seems to be a sense of dissatisfaction with what was already there. [Pause]

Participant 1: What does it mean to believe?

Facilitator: What does it mean to believe? What is that rooted in? How do we come to belief?

Participant 1: I can't believe - all these words in this description are pretty ambivalent - Destroy Mercilessly - I don't believe that's what's meant. I think that what it means is that by acceptance, by accepting something, I've destroyed it. So by not feeding it, I destroy it. But I have to accept it first. So I can't take something out and dispense with it without causing some kind of problem. So

I destroy it by using intelligence to accept it. By accepting it, it loses its power over me. For instance, (tape unclear....) So I can't believe it's a violent process.

Facilitator: Do you mean that we have to accept that this has been put into us?

Participant 1: I cannot speak for the rest of the world. I can only speak for myself. But obviously through my life in whatever event it is, I realize something is lopsided and I must accept this in my life. I work on myself and 'work on myself' means, in part, that I must accept that I am all my thoughts, my feelings, all my life circumstances. I accept that because that's what I am and that's what I must work with. So by working with them I accept them. I can doff my hat to them. If I doff my hat to them it means that I'm not attacking them. It means the more I doff my hat to them, the less reactive I become to words, the less power they have over me.

Facilitator: So, something in us becomes separated from the beliefs and views?

Participant 1: Yes, because I create something that separates itself from 'me' and it views or observes me or whatever I am. So if I suppress something I am less than honest because suppressing something that could be observed and accepted [unclear] ... and if God can't accept me as I am, impartially, then ... [unclear].

Participant 2: How does the text relate to Gurdjieff's method of destruction? How do you see that?

Participant 1: Because I can. It has to do with subjectivity - all my personality, thoughts and feelings are subjective.

Participant 2: I just wanted to ask [P #1] - I understand how you speak of the process because G. says in his text the aim of this text is to destroy and he uses quite violent terms. I want to know how that relates to the text - to G's method of destruction. How do you see that relative to the text?

Participant 1: We've isolated a part of the text obviously. But I think my reaction to this is that it's all very violent and I don't think work on me myself is violent. I may have to do something, use a more aggressive method in order to get them to come forth live because the more I attack them its like throwing oil on them. I don't believe that a violent attack on my .....

Participant 2: No - I understand that. But Gurdjieff says the aim of this is to destroy and he uses quite violent terms. I do understand that.

[Interchange is quite unclear]

Participant 1: G. will destroy mercilessly - by acceptance.

truths are seen as falsehoods by Gurdjieff. Further, - the destruction is focused on beliefs and views "about *everything* existing in the World". There is no qualification here - it is 'everything'!

How (are) we to understand the words 'destroy' are, 'corrode' and 'extirpate'? Gurdjieff was well aware of the etymological significance of words and apparently gave considerable attention to the English words used in the translation of *Beelzebub's Tales*. The present availability of the Russian text of the "*Tales*" makes it possible to compare and analyze a host of words, widening the 'horizon of meaning' and enriching the "inner content" of many passages. In this regard Nicholas Tereshchenko's knowledge of Russian has been a valuable resource, one that we have called on frequently.

In answer to queries about the Russian meaning and etymology of 'destroy', 'corrode', 'mercilessly' and 'rubbish' Nic stated the following:

"The old-fashioned word Mister Gurdjieff uses in the front page and again on the first page of the last chapter is a very interesting one. Its primary meaning is "to eat away all the grass", like by cattle put out to graze. It's derived, secondary, meaning is "to corrode something", "to cauterize (a wound for infection)", and has also been used (in the proper context) to mean "set the dogs" on to someone (with the intention to have him killed). Finally, it shares its root (which, by itself; simply means "grass" or "herb") with the verb "to poison".

The Russian word [bezposhchadno] translated as "mercilessly" can mean: unsparingly, mercilessly, unmercifully, inexorably, harshly, and cruelly. And the word [khlam] translated as 'rubbish' means: odds and ends, remains, rubbish, lumber, anything old and become useless."

The English words 'destroy', and 'corrode' seem to have been approved by Gurdjieff because, together, they broaden the meaning considerably and offer alternatives which, when blended together, communicate more subtle aspects of a three brained image that is analogous to mentation by form.

In English, 'destroy' means (1) to ruin utterly (2) consume or dissolve (3) to tear down, demolish or raze (4) to put an end to; to make useless [L. de - down + struere - to arrange, construct].

Corrode, in English, means (1) to eat away gradually, as by chemical action (2) to destroy, consume or impair (3) gradual breakdown by surface disintegration. [L. corrodese com - thoroughly: rodese - to gnaw].

Extirpate, the term chosen by the editors of the 1974 edition, means (1) to root out or up, to destroy wholly, to exterminate or abolish. [L. ex - out *plus* stirps - stem or root].

When brought together, in the context of Gurdjieff's stated intention "to destroy, mercilessly..." and "to corrode without mercy all the rubbish accumulated during the ages in human mentation"[2], we are faced with a multifaceted *process* with many nuances of meaning.

Our first topic for discussion will surround the questions 'How do *you* understand "to destroy and to corrode"? And, 'What is the nature of that process/event'?

The second topic for discussion concerns the specific 'beliefs and views' that are to be destroyed or corroded. How does one destroy a belief or view in one's mentation and feelings? What are these rooted beliefs and views? Is Gurdjieff referring to all the religious and philosophical teachings that have been present for centuries? To all scientific and occult views and beliefs? Or, is he referring to those deeper and more fundamental views and beliefs that lie within the traditions and philosophies, views and beliefs that concern the nature of reality, of consciousness, of man's purpose and biologically-given states? If his aim concerns these more deeply held views and beliefs, then how does that influence our comprehension of the teachings of the Great Traditions and Philosophies? In the end the question, "What is to take its place in 'beliefs and views'?", remains in front of us. How do these new beliefs and views take form in our mentation and feelings? In what way or ways do we verify them?

© Copyright 2001 - Keith Buzzell - All Rights Reserved

---

[2] P.p. 1184 'From the Author'

Participant 3: The thought that comes to me is that we destroy mercilessly a particular belief by converting that belief into doubt. It is no longer a belief so, in effect, we destroy that belief but you haven't destroyed the concept of whatever it is. That's what you said?

Participant 1: Then I'm free, I'm no longer up walled.

Participant 4: I think he (G) is presenting us with an image of an ongoing process. I don't see the violence so much as that we are continually taking out the roots of what has become a living problem on our earth. We are told in our (so called roots), in our total upbringing and experiences, to believe and expect. We all have our little beliefs, rules, thought processes, prejudices etc. It is ongoing - I get the image that these roots may again sprout things that will be problems. Mr. G. is asking us to carry on a continual self-examination of our thought processes and what we are doing to each other on a continual basis. It isn't just a one time situation where you read the *"Tales"* once and perceive that everything that has gone on is wrong, and then proceed to push it aside as rubbish. It's a continual effort as he said so nicely "effort-effort-effort". We won't really 'succeed'.

Facilitator: So the image here, arising from the etymology of the words, this picturing by word (thought), feeling and sensation this is what I found of profound significance. This is a way of approaching Three Brained Being's - to always have thinking, sensation, feeling and action in mind. So the image of rooting out, of stems, of grass growing- of it being nibbled on - but then, from another perspective, of being extirpated, rooted out and thrown away - a much more active thing; and their corrosion - a surface thing - a chemical action on the surface - and that's a very different thing from pulling it out. So there are all of these images, these sensations, of gouging and pulling it out etc., so there are picturings that are communicating the inner content of the process.

Participant 4: The genius or beauty of this book is that you can attempt to do the process that he is asking you to do in many different ways. You don't have to do it in a totally intellectual process or a totally emotional or physical process. You certainly don't have to do it as a totally emotional or physical process... I think he's asking us to get rid of all these things any which way we individually can.

Participant 1: You're seeing it as a non-violent process - someone else was trying to steer you to do it as a violent process - you are doing it as if looking at it objectively - that is part of getting rid of it. He is giving us all of that in one sentence.

Participant 5: In response to your first thought - the idea of mentation by thought and mentation by form. There are so many things in the book - things that strike me differently. One, for example, is his impact on animal sacrifice. He goes into it for me very logically. What's the sense of killing two brained beings for the benefit of His Endlessness - it makes no intellectual sense at all. The other thing which seems for me to go for mentation by form or strikes my emotion is when he calls a great leader a vainglorious Greek that strikes me as emotional because it doesn't explain intellectually but I feel it. I don't know a whole lot about that.

Participant 2: First of all I think this destruction is not about our destruction. This is Gurdjieff saying 'He is making destruction', and his next book [*Meetings with Remarkable Men*] is the Creation of suitable material. But what I propose is that he has methods of destroying this kind of mentation and one is by contradiction. For instance he mentioned animal sacrifice. In half of the book Gurdjieff is saying that animal sacrifice is bad and bad results follow from it, but then later he says, in reference to the First World War that there wasn't enough. He contradicts both points of view. He has a lot of contradictions in this book. He says right at the beginning that he is very good at muddling and befuddling. I think it's good to concentrate on how does he use the text to be destructive? The other thing is that his phrase is almost an exact quote from Madame Blavatsky's phrase in the *Secret Doctrine*.

Facilitator: What was the specific reference?

Participant 2: The bit where Gurdjieff says he's going to sweep away, to destroy all of the rubbish. That is almost a direct quote of something which is in the *Secret Doctrine*. So I'm just saying that because we're looking at the particular meaning of the word - that seems to be connected to it.

Participant 6: I have 3 things to say in addition to what has been spoken about. First - it seems totally logical to me that if you want to learn something new you must sweep away the old. It's like the old saying, "You can't fill a glass of water when it's already full". Anyone in a meditation process, whatever study it is, should create a space with a sense of humour whether that be for information, practical knowledge or whatever. A new identity should be ready, should have a sensing of where we can put the new material. The second is that when G. talks about destroying, he talks about death - the death somehow or other for me - the keynote is the teaching that there will be life only if we die to ourselves. The third - People who taught me the Work, who were with Gurdjieff a long time once told me the Gurdjieff himself instructed them by saying (I quote as best I can) 'It is necessary in the Work at a given moment to disregard everything - throw away all conceptions that you have - literally everything!'

Participant 7: How it strikes me - at the beginning of the book - as a statement of intent - for me in reading the book I found myself in many different parts of myself I remember feeling very embarrassed, in others very confused, and even at different times. The first and second times I read a certain section that also was different. One time I was maybe embarrassed, another time maybe disgusted. So what I hear from the etymology of what you're saying - when you talked about nibbling the grass or uprooting something - how I understand that is what his words by form are creating in me at different times. Sometimes I felt violence. I had not already read the whole book. Through the exercise of the Work my patience became better. For almost a year I felt void and almost angry because I wasn't taught to think. I was very confused. Nothing interested me and I didn't know if this Work was good or if it was useful for other people and if I was just angry. I remember being angry at night because it had no reality. It took almost a year for me to discover that this reality was more real than the other. Then it was wonderful.

Participant 8: For me Gurdjieff means precisely what he says in that paragraph. I think that Gurdjieff knows that man is made in the image of God and what it implies for man as a possible host for a guest, which might be God, for want of a better metaphor. That it is inevitable given his roots in the Universe which in itself was made in the image of God. That man will go through phases which on the one hand they have to be reached and on the other hand they have to be transcended. The first phase is not to constrain a man in a certain duality with the rest of the Universe. Gurdjieff emphasizes that there are places where a man must divide in himself and it seems to me that those are the places which are the most law conformingly appropriate to give up to the possibility of a new phase.

(Side #1 of the tape ends - commentary by Participant 8 is incomplete)

Participant 1: …if necessary… the other end of the stick in ourselves, to be able to discover anything and everything in ourselves with the confidence that it will be immediately replaced in some pure way.

Facilitator: There is an additional question I wanted to consider. It has to do with the focus on mentation and feeling. One should say that this is the thought process and the feelings process. But he does not mention the action process. He does not mention destroying in the body – and I think that this is an interesting and maybe important thing. His focus is on mentation, upon thinking (views) and feelings. But he doesn't say anything about the physical body.

Participant 3: for me it brings me to a stage at which I have real emotion but virtually all the knowledge that I have is not real knowledge. What I know is that the Sun will rise tomorrow, but until it does, that is not really knowledge.

Facilitator: This seems to be pointing in the direction of verifying somehow or other that we can come much closer to what is real and that has a mentation, a thought process that is consistent with feeling, consistent with physical action. In other words, if we say something about love, or about sharing, this is a word, an abstraction, but there is the feeling state and there must be the action. This is a three-brain thing. So often we get lost in the words, in the definitions. One of the things that Mr. Gurdjieff is trying to help us see here is that it's not like that. That's what I was talking about when I spoke about a 'disconnected abstraction'. It has no relation to anything unless it has a resonance in us in the world of feeling and an equivalent resonance in the action itself, which would be a manifestation of the word that we are talking about. It has to have all three in order for it to be real. For instance, that would be the 'picturings' that Gurdjieff was talking about when he talks about the Transcaucasian Kurd, his grandmother, or Hadji Asvatz Troov and creates this tremendous unfolding of image that has a connection to all three of our parts. That creates something that words alone would be powerless to accomplish. They would be just disconnected abstraction.

Participant 5: Just as in the experience of Self awareness it's more complete if one can bring all three parts to it. It's still useful when we bring two parts to it and even if we can't relate it to the action. If we can somehow think it or feel it, it can be very strong.

Participant 9: I want to comment more specifically on the last question on why the physical is not spoken of. It seems to me that biological evolution has pretty much taken care of the physical body and they function in many aspects in which we have no control and no awareness. Certainly we all talk about digestion. We can sense digestion to some degree, but I can't sense taking apart molecules and connecting up proteins in the digestive part of my body. So it seems that the physical body will take care of itself. For the most part it has its systems set up and those systems will move in us. They can be very heavily influenced by the second and third brain. So if we will work with the second and third brain in these ideas which we are presenting – to destroy mercilessly etc. – those are the areas that we can actually get at if you have an [unclear?] impression and they will in their turn take care of the body and make appropriate changes as it is needed. I'm not sure if I'm making myself clear. For example, digestion, the immune process, health and disease, change in blood pressure, those kinds of things.

Facilitator: Would you say that that is analogous to the Purgatory chapter where Gurdjieff says in the outflow of the 'automatic creation' is the appearance of Tetartocosmos, of the 'automatic independent motion on the surface of the planet'. Now, this is a physical body able to move automatically, but independently. This is now a life form that has the ability and has put into it this first octave, the octave of food. This is given from Above, already guided by the thrust of Theomertmalogos (high cosmic law). That is the resonance with what you were saying. But Gurdjieff clearly separates that from what comes later when he speaks about the invention. He doesn't call it an intervention, rather that Endlessness, seeing the verification in the appearance of that automatic independent motion, then actualizes everything necessary. What follows is the appearance of the second and third (feeling and thinking) brain *in potential*. The first, the physical body, guided by high cosmic law, is already complete. Everything beyond that is there in potential. They appear, from the world of possibilities, throughout history – the best of them, in three brained beings deriving from the Great Traditions and Philosophies. But they become crystallized – rigid over time. When I observe those beliefs and views in myself, all coming from the past, I see that they are *not* mine, they are 'automatized'. They have come from my parents, my teachers, the society etc. I did not come to them myself. They are the beliefs and views rooted in us by centuries. Then it is not a question of whether they are good or bad, for me it is more a question that they are not mine. They are 'automatized' in me. I am not truly aware of them…

Participant 10: I create a compromise. Everything you said and the good and the bad from the past – centuries of the traditions and attempts to reawaken are coming from the outside and I try to live with both of them in harmony. I create a harmony as best as I can, which is actually quite a lot of disharmony, and this all happens in the intellectual and emotional realm, the second totality, which is what compromises of truth, when that compromise includes all of False Personality, Inner Considering etc. which all exist in that totality?

Participant 11: In *Life is Real* Gurdjieff describes three totalities within the psyche of man. The first is mentation by form. It is the accumulated experience from the instinctive and moving center. We know this is because he repeatedly spoke of it. The second totality is the totality of meaning – the emotional and the intellectual centre. We receive these [nine] influences – these inputs – and build these structures in which the emotional centre is the 'backing up' – its forces standing behind those [things]. Gurdjieff also described a third totality which is the voluntary contact between these first two totalities. The contemplation, of what he called logical confrontation. I think what he is trying to do with the book, particularly since he describes three ways of reading it – the first depending on mentation by form, then mentation by subjective [?] meaning only. Then you try to understand. What he is trying to get us to do is to use that third totality, however weakly developed it may be within us, to create and see the logical confrontations between the beliefs we have accumulated and to eat away at the certainty, at the emotional force we have put behind the beliefs, to the point where we can take them and use them almost impartially, and at least try to verify these previously held [? secrets]

Facilitator: Yesterday some of us spent some time talking about the 'objective impartial criticisms' and this seems to be connected to something that had to do with a high mental function. (The objectivity). The impartiality having to do with an inner attitude, a state having to do with our 'Being' world. Is there a possible analogy between that and what you have just said?

Participant 11: Yes. The Higher Emotional Intellectual Center which John showed on the top story [unclear] … because we don't listen to what is coming down, we just listen to our intentions and meaning gets focused in the middle story in what we know to be true because we heard in son many places. We don't create the energy to let those impressions up to the higher emotional center or when we do in a situation where we have fallen into a belief system or it has been forced upon us by religious institution.

Facilitator: So we have these crystallizations or these coalescences of beliefs and views. How much time do we have left? –Laughter- 3 min. We perhaps can open the door a bit to the process itself. How does one take apart a belief or a view" Realistically, how is this accomplished? How do you see this?

Participant 11: Gurdjieff does describe that in the chapter Holy Purgatory where he describes the process of confrontation between the results of the Cosmic Laws and the expectations of man's so called 'sane logic'. And what he is talking about is to take what you have in your second totality [from your sane logic] and compare it with what you can actually perceive, how you verify your sane logic using your ability to contemplate.

Facilitator: This turns out to be very useful for me. It is the process of verification and of rebuilding whatever is going to take the place of what we've destroyed. This is built on this 'three brained process'. The confrontative logic must involve all of these three brains, whatever form of mentation, thought or feeling process and actions or physical manifestations are concerned. It is the constancy of bringing these up against each other and comparing, evaluation – because the one powerful way we have of testing the reality of whatever it is we put in front of us is to put it in front of all three brains. Is it logical, consistent, does it resonate with our emotional world of relationship and when it gets out there in mentation, is it possible? Only when there is a resonance here do we begin to get a taste of what Gurdjieff refers to with his 'sensation picturings', which is the whole underpinning of communication in the *Tales*. He teaches always by giving three brained images – always. There is something magical there that is not present in most of the world's literature. Most literature is disconnected abstraction, thinking or it is feeling divorced from the intellect or physical manifestation. The fact that they are not whole, that they are fragmented, is one of the points that separate it from the *Tales*.

Well we are out of time. Thank you!

End of Session

Seminar 3 - Chapter 6 & 7 of Beelzebub's Tales

Facilitator: Tony Blake

At the Invitation of the planning committee Mr. Anthony Blake and his colleague, Ms. Karen Stefano was invited to the All & Everything Conference to facilitate one afternoon's seminars. As an experiment in an alternative approach to our seminars exploring *Beelzebub's Tales*, Mr. Blake was invited to introduce the conference participants to a process named Logovisual Technology (LVT). Due to the nature of LVT, as will become evident, a full direct transcription of the afternoon's discussions is not possible. What is presented below is intended to give a reasonably accurate flavour of the seminars. LVT is introduced followed by a brief narrative description of the process as carried through the remainder of the day. Both afternoons seminars are represented below in one segment. Mr. Blake is the designated facilitator. Further information on LVT may be found on the Duversity web site at www.duversity.org

Facilitator: What we are going to be doing is slightly experimental it will be the application of a technique which is beginning to be used through various regions of management, more than in any other area. It's a method of thinking together. We might possibly agree, at least in general terms, that thinking together is problematic. Thinking is usually a process which tends to be isolationist or often exercised in opposition to other people on the basis of argument so that to find some way that people can actually join together, bring together, elements of thought to construct something of greater worth than they could, at least individually, might be advantageous.

I always remember one of the very striking Sufi stories told by Idries Shah of the three dervishes seeking for the truth, one of whom is looking for the deeper knowledge. And he accesses the deeper knowledge by standing in a well and finding a mirror composed of all the fragments of thought of humanity; just about coherent enough to reflect the deeper knowledge. And the problem was to image the fragments to foster an appreciation of seeing the whole. As far as I am concerned the general rule in that of human process is the more people you put together the stupider they are and that any one of us in this room could be a rational sane being, but put us into a group working something out together and the result is mostly that of the proverbial camel designed by [a committee...?].

But with all of these apologia etc., etc.; this particular technique I've given the name Logovisual technology (LVT). I'll split it down into three parts; logo; meaning the word, visual; making it seen or apparent, and technology; in part referring to it being tangible and movable.

So this is a process whereby thoughts are made apparent, visible but also in a form that we can handle and move as an option. So instead of them being locked up inside some mysterious process which we generally call thought, which is a very strange internal process, we are working in terms of explicit material which is visible to all and which we can actually experiment with. We have simple tools which enable us to mimic it. You know, as with any technique, the less you are aware of the technique the more effective it is. You spend your time being aware of the technique and you end up going round in an eternal circle. Like Wim would say about a true pianist; when he plays a piece, if it sounds difficult when he is playing it, he is not playing it right. It should sound as natural as falling water. So with that proviso most of you are seeing something that is unfamiliar and may be saying "what the hell is this and how do I do it" thus interfering in the process. Hopefully, you will be experienced enough to relax and not let this worry you. I will just add one more thing, that this particular technique I took from ideas which now date back almost forty years to researches at Bennett's (I was with him at the time, during the sixties) having to do with education and how to facilitate the educational process.

Now on to the particular theme we will be addressing. We will be working together in a specific pattern so that most of the time I'm going to ask you to split into three groups. Now to the task at hand. I have been told that we will address/process chapters six and seven of *Beelzebub's Tales*. Is this correct? I propose, for the sake of this exercise to treat the two chapters together. I am assuming that you have read the chapters and know them pretty thoroughly. Say we are a group presented with this task of, I'll use some verb such as reflecting on, to understand, or to deal with, the material of these chapters. We want to find a starting point we can agree on amongst ourselves so as to proceed with the exercise. In LVT it is important to spend a little time to say what might be the question we could generate or address concerning these two chapters in front of us. For instance; "what do these two chapters have to say about the nature of immortality?" No question, no process. As Mr. G. was want to say; unless you have a burning question you don't get nowhere. No question; what is the point of an answer?

So let's talk about it. What kind of question do you want to ask about it besides "what the hell do they mean?"

Participant 1: That is the question! What is it really about; what is he telling us?

Facilitator: Why does he include the comments on perpetual motion?

Participant 1: He made a lot of sense but he didn't answer these questions. What's perpetual motion all about? He didn't answer that.

Facilitator: That might have been a kindness on his part. So why perpetual motion?

Participant 2: The possible connection to the previous chapters that may be related to that?

Facilitator: You mean the previous comments about the forms of space travel?

Seminar 3 - Chapter 6 & 7 of Beelzebub's Tales

Participant 2: Yes, the forms of space travel.

Facilitator: Could you attempt to formulate a question?

Participant 2: Do the changes in the various forms of space travel, however allegorical we may see them, tell us something about , or have something to do with, the continuing process suggested by perpetual motion?

Participant 3: Before we can ask or answer that we have to come to a consensus as to what we understand space travel to mean.

Facilitator: In these exercises we have to have a reasonable starting point with what we can (Do) in a reasonable span of time. Perhaps I could interpret what you say in terms of;
What do we understand by space travel in the context of these chapters?

Participant 3: Yes.

Facilitator: Any more suggestions? (Pause...long pause, very long pause)

Participant 4: There is a clear relationship between the previous chapters that have to do with the space drives to chapter six. There is not such a clear connection between chapter 6 and 7. What would be the interior resonances between chapters 6 and 7? That would be my question.

Facilitator: Yes. We have a couple of slightly different questions. Can we hold these in mind? Any more?

Participant: [at this point several statements were made which were inaudible]

Participant 5: Why the apparent objection to external resources?

Facilitator: We now have a different spread of questions. Before we proceed we have to have a sufficient consensus without voting. Before proceeding could I ask that we hear from some of you who have not spoken to give their ideas on the preferred questions?

Participant: [several inaudible responses]

Facilitator: So we have a focus on perpetual motion, on the connection between the chapters, another on the placement of the chapters in the sequence of the book, what else? Participant 6: The space drives.

Participant 7: Why does he give us a past in chapter seven in relation to this material?

89

Participant 8: I would ask "what is the connection or relationship between genuine-being-duty and perpetual motion?"

Facilitator: Well, because we are short of time and are in something of an artifice here I will impose my will upon you and suggest that we take this question, but this is my imposition on you. Could you repeat that question?

Participant 8: What is the relationship between genuine-being-duty and perpetual motion?

Facilitator: In this process I have to be rather didactic and say "you go away and do 'x' and then we will come back together and do 'y'. So, we will keep to a strict time table. We have two kinds of resources. We have the text itself and we have what I would call in mental terms our associations to the text; whatever we have from the other parts of the book or other things we know. What I need you to do next is to consider putting forward the ingredients for an answer to this question. What are the significant elements of answering this question? You can choose to do this in terms of itemizing or in terms of some insight you have. Now we go into the mechanics of this because a tool is a technology. I want you to split into three groups, as I said before each of you will have a set of tools. One will be this board [a white magnetic board] and the other will be a set of these [small, yellow, magnetic hexagons]. As you're in your group you generate the ingredients relating to the question. Many people, each one of you, can make a statement and of course the space within which you will write [on the yellow hexagons, see Figure 1.] won't allow you to use too many words. So you could say something like "the use of a special container". Put it up on the board. Don't make any order out of it or arrange it in any way. Write clearly so that everyone in the group knows what is meant. Place the hexagons like this [see Figure 1 below]. Don't use single words; make a statement. Allow yourselves to play! As soon as you place these on the board it is like depositing them in an artificial mind-bank.

The above represents what material could be transcribed from the afternoon's meetings. Following in figures 1 through 3, are initial material generated by groups 1, 2 and 3 respectively.

These were the elemental statements which formed the initial input into the proposed question "what is the relationship between genuine-being-duty and perpetual motion?"

After the groups spent some time generating these elements and placing them at random on each groups board each group was then instructed to consider how all these separate elements might fit together into larger wholes. Perhaps a number of elements shared common characteristics such that a grouping could be formed and given a new designation. This process of playing with the various elements to see what larger concepts where inferred was represented visually with green magnetic circles. When a group was satisfied that a larger block of meaning existed a new designation was given it and this was written on the green circle (Figure 4.) Each of the three separate groups of people went through this process as a group. Figure 4 is a picture of the results of group 2. These steps in the process for groups 1 and 3 have been omitted in the following figures. The results of groups 1 and 3 can be inferred from the final figure (Figure 5). Upon completion of the process just described all three groups came back together again. Each group brought back with them the green circles as described above and all were then placed together on a single board (Figure 5). The whole group then looked together and experimented with different manners of relating all these new categories of meaning described in the circles. Figure 5 merely represents the final position of the circles when the afternoon seminar was ended. Previously, the circles had been arranged in an anagrammatic form, in the form of the "tree of life" and many connections within the various forms were suggested.

End of Session

All & Everything Conference 2001

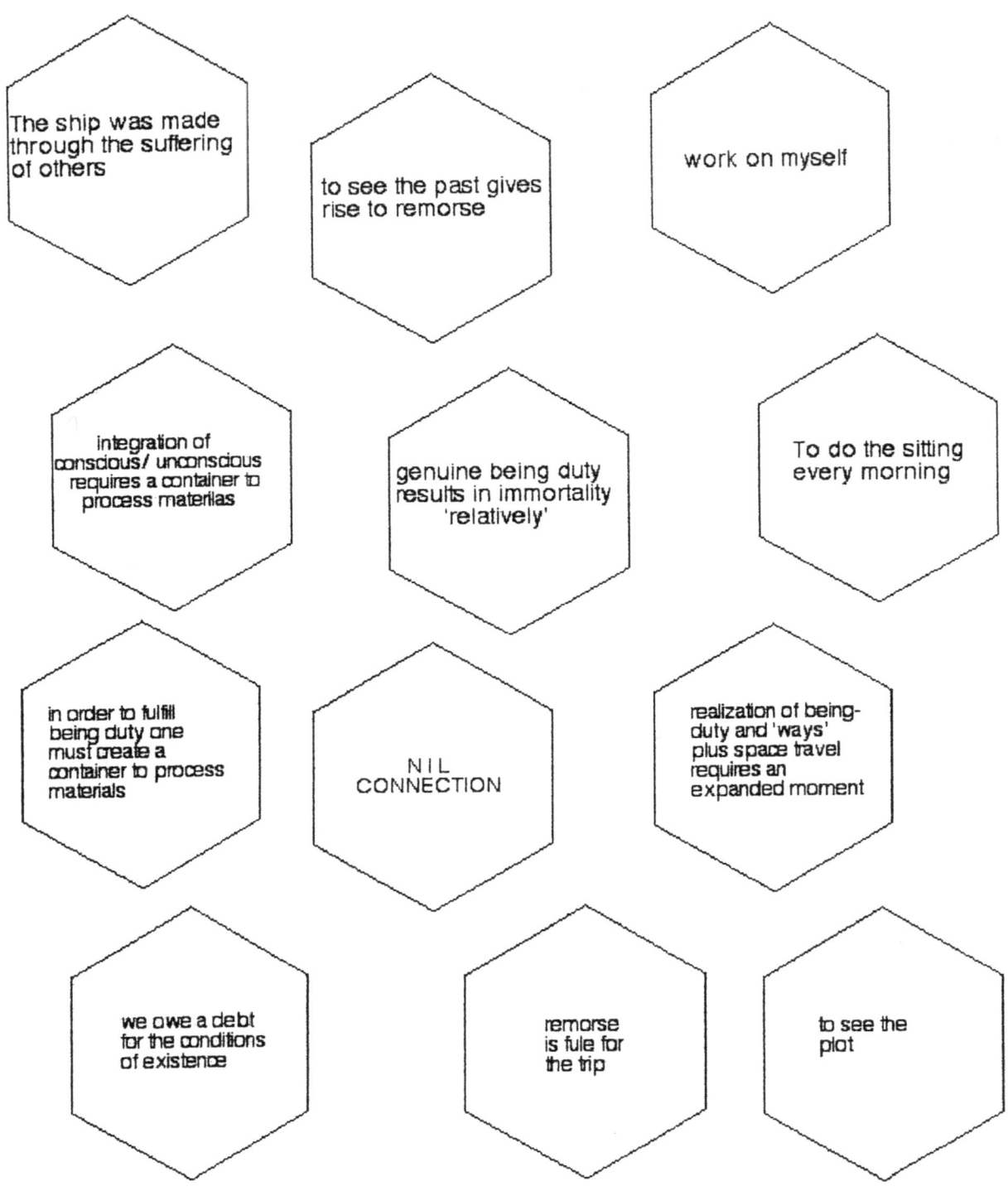

Figure 1. Group 1

Seminar 3 - Chapter 6 & 7 of Beelzebub's Tales

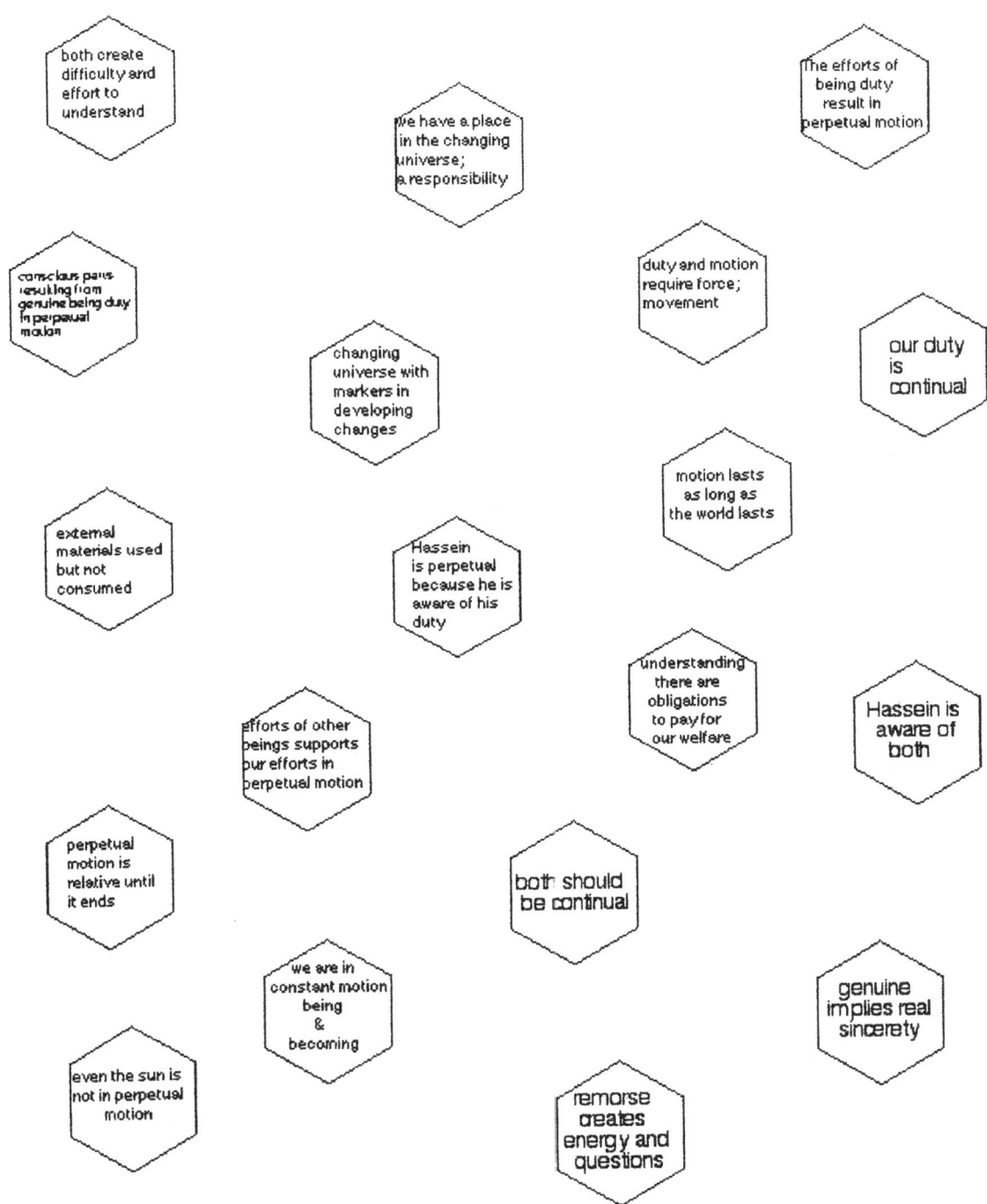

Figure 2. Group 2

All & Everything Conference 2001

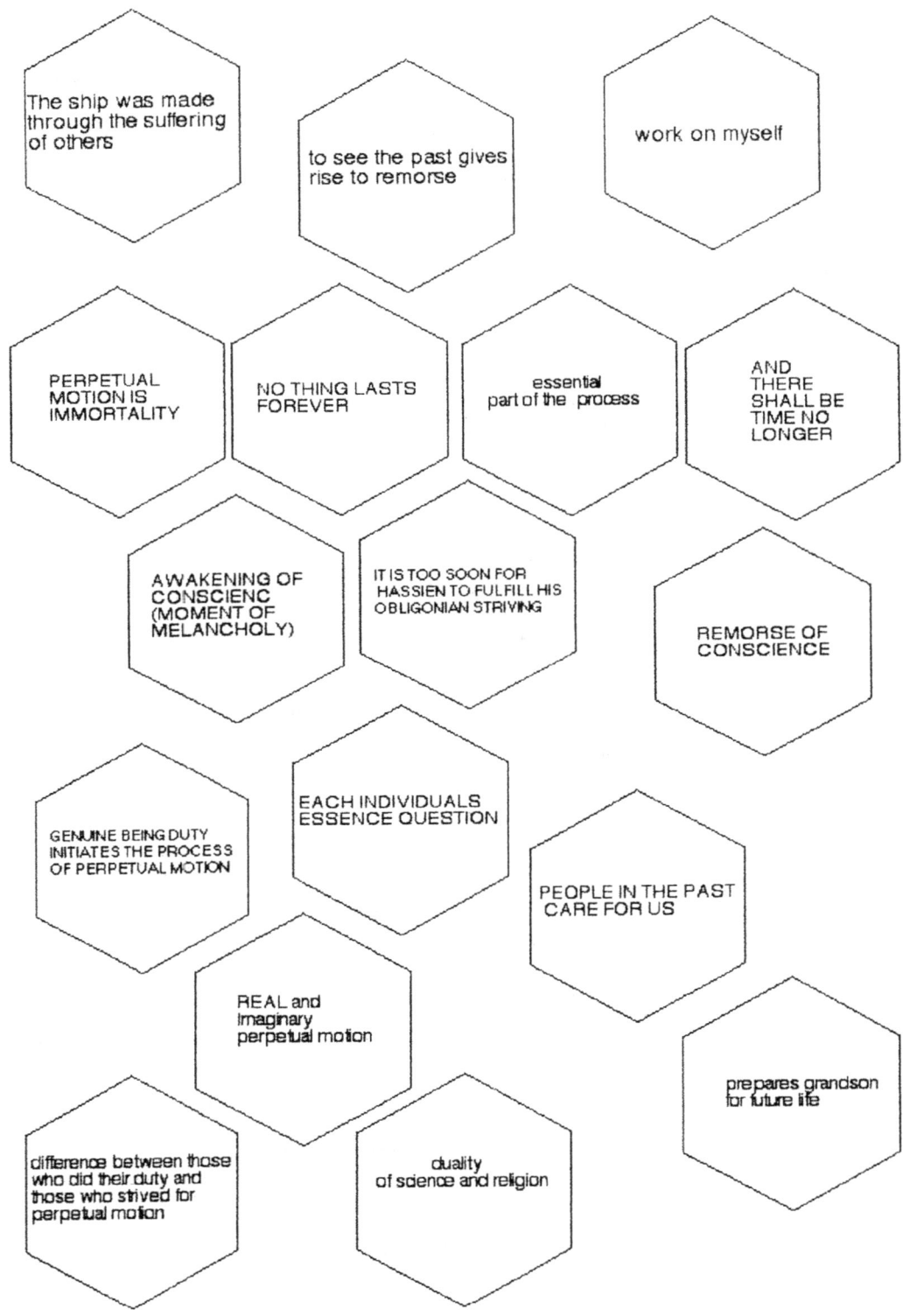

Figure 3. Group 3

Seminar 3 - Chapter 6 & 7 of Beelzebub's Tales

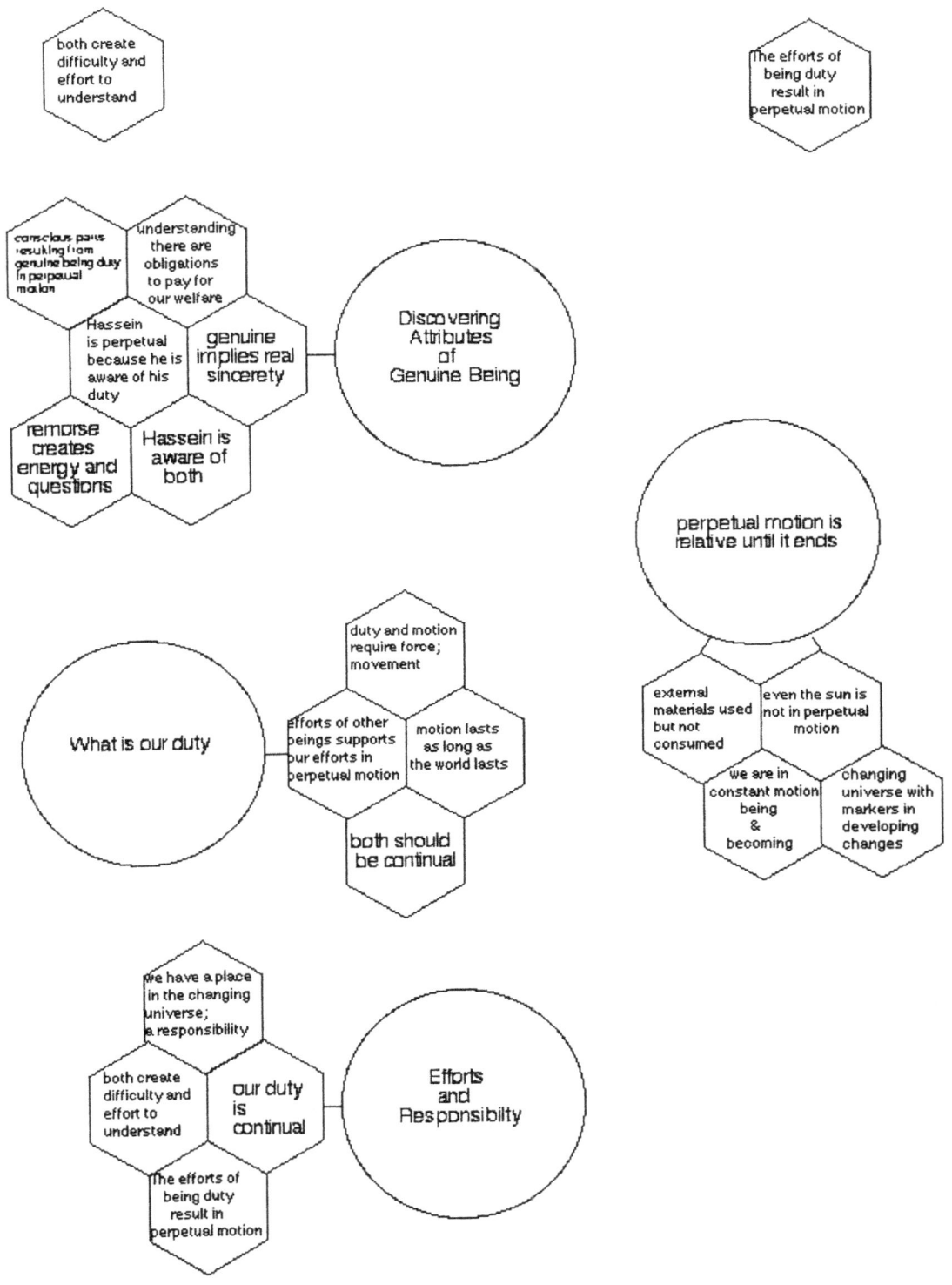

Figure 4.

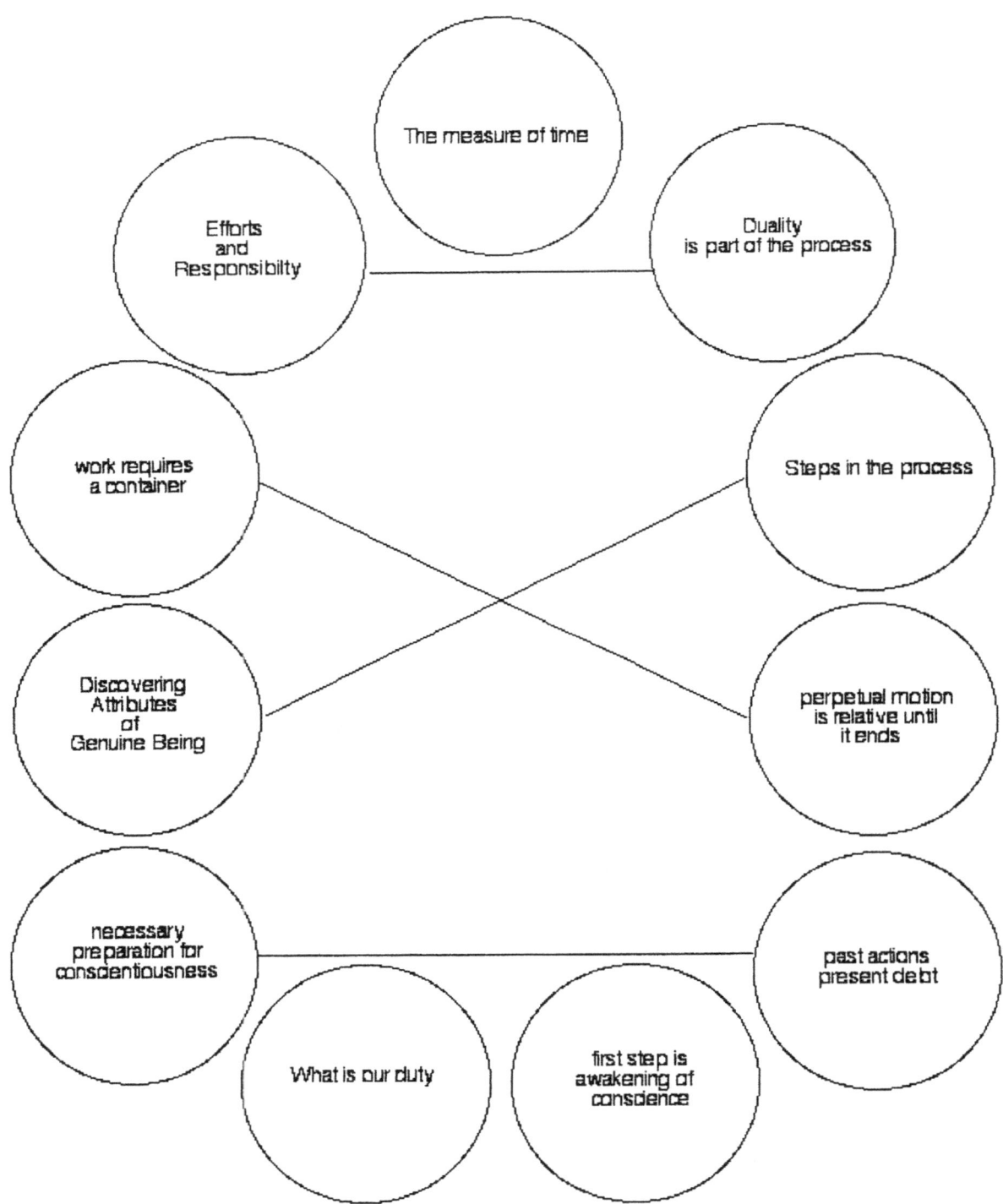

Figure 5. All Groups Combined

Duversity

Tony Blake

First I promise [unclear] will be pleased to know that I do not propose to talk for very long, are you pleased about that?

I propose to split this session into two parts the first one a kind of a spiel and the second an opportunity to experiment with [unclear] which some of you may find interesting. First to comment on Duversity, the name of this organization. First a brief comment on the genesis of this strange name. This began many years ago when I was with Mr. Bennett and some of you will know that he wrote a monumental tome called The Dramatic Universe. I thought this was a very good start and one day there ought to be a Dramatic University so that was the genesis of the D University the Dramatic University. [unclear] And then it became in time something else, the foreign characteristic of... Let me backtrack a bit before I start. I have to say that one of the things that attracted me about Bennett's work was it was all inclusive but not conclusive. That is to say he preferred, and Bennett introduced, this sphere of being that one could at best get a kind of progressive approximation to what was really going on. There was no such thing as having a direct blueprint being got from heaven into your lap which would actually give you the answers to what was going on for good or ill. You were stuck with finding out constantly finding out, trying to find out as best you could. The proposition was at the close of the nineteenth century which was the last heyday of the great Philosophical systems Dr. Hegel as Kierkegaard pointed out produces wonderful great edifices like palaces [unclear] and then personally lived in a shack at the bottom of the garden that is where he actually lived had nothing to do with the system he produced.

I am going to look at it not in terms however of a grand design, grand blueprint I referred to just now but in terms of ourselves. We are rapidly seeing that in all areas of human endeavour the sort of model portrayed or demonstrated by science was becoming more the kind of guideline we can possibly hope to follow and to [include together], co-operate , to look into areas of experience and come to provisional formulations and [unclear] ... reformulations.. [unclear] and we sense no end to it. His own book TDU he accepted as the set of footnotes on A&E he comments on aspects of [unclear] that incredible, great work but unfortunately many people then took what he had then written, and it was always in the spirit of exploration, as his own version of 'the gospel' and to be quoted as providing answers to every question you had ever [never?] thought of asking. Which like so many of these things are [unclear] the answers which people devour without ever having asked the question.

All & Everything Conference 2001

He wanted to make a transition to a world in which we accepted fundamental uncertainty, incompleteness. In doing so he was paralleling other parts of the 'zeitgeist' and recently we begin to understand more and more that mathematics is largely chaotic and undecidable and not at all the ground of firm absolute invariant truths at all!, and if this happens in mathematics you can be sure it will be prevalent everywhere else. Unfortunately things which happen in such areas take [unclear – four -?] hundred years to penetrate into the general human thinking. Bennett instilled that this was, or he believed this was going to take place in the sphere which is to do with "higher matters" all of the prevalence of the sense that there was some kind of universally understood principle governing the spiritual reality, that it, this itself would be called into question. So our notions of say, Aldous Huxley's Perennial Philosophy [unclear] in a very small cultural [unclear] is nothing but a wishful projection. This I absorbed not quite with my mother's milk but in my first years, so to speak, it became part of my attitude towards things. But I began to see that this idea of a Dramatic University which could so easily be turned into a way of propagating a different man's ideas, that is, Bennett's ideas needed to be gone into even more deeply. And in particular that there was hinted at if not really all that clearly expressed that there was hinted at within in his work and some of the [unclear] including I would say for myself Gurdjieff a very profound shift to follow and following [unclear] and that is, [Oh hello Gang! Oh of course, pot-lucky! Come and sit down. Just getting to the nub of it.]

I think I can best express this [unclear] because one of the features of what I am interested in with Karen is forming a kind of working fusion between things which have developed in certain areas of psychology and certain things which we have received from [unclear] the occult tradition. But one of the present contemporary people whom we are friends with [unclear] is a man called Gordon Lawrence who worked for a long time with an organization called The Tavistock Institute which is based in London and has a long history going from, goes back to the time of the Second World War where the first studies were being made into 'Group Process' and this is absolutely crucial. [unclear] Some of you any of you who know anything about the Tavistock Institute of Human Relations and the enormous researches that they have done over the years on group process will know that one of the key ideas around fifty years ago [centre on?] [Dijon and?] who were the pioneers of articulating what happens in groups of people. And there were very, and even in those times and there were some very interesting questions to be raised about the history em, let's talk about how the conditions under which you can get your people in a work group, you mean it in the fourth way but it is still relevant in a work group, that is, people who can actually co-operate [unclear - agree on a task?] and accomplish them that most human groupings tend to have authority in which they ostensibly gather together to co-operate on a task but they fall into some kind of let's call It [unclear] a self-deception part of the, the main part of the self-deception mean that refers to the idea that in these people's opinion nearly every group which meets together believes that it is immortal and that there is always tomorrow. So this is another version of Gurdjieff's 'disease of tomorrow'. It had a very, very profound effect on human grouping.

And also the group begins to manifest processes in itself which have nothing to do with accomplishing the task whatsoever but to do with perpetuating itself [unclear]. At least that is a very fascinating area and I would recommend anyone reading the classic Dijon's Experiences in

Groups which is one of first real empirical studies of what happens when groups of groups of people meet together. [unclear] Anyway from that tradition there came those groups of people who argue immensely among themselves with one group of them have dealt with the following distinction and they use the term ['unclear] and they mean something like the forces governing the group process and they distinguish between two kinds of politics, the politics of salvation, and they are using this terminology in a very special way, and the politics of revelation. Now understand, these kinds of labels and descriptions are going into [unclear - any kind of a group?] or commercial organization, it can be a church or a sports club, any kind of grouping whatsoever, they can call themselves spiritual, or they can call themselves atheist, it doesn't matter this is to do with all kinds of human groupings. [unclear] ...behind all this is that any, what happens when groups of people get together is what happens when groups of people get together! [unclear]

I have found this distinction very useful it is neither polemical nor argumentative. In the politics of salvation the group looks for its salvation, the resolution of its problems, that would be problems of understanding, the problem of being whatever problems that they feel they have [unclear] look for it being resolved by something coming from outside to resolve them. So it is like, in a sense, a caricature of waiting for Jesus Christ to drop in and do it for you. And also of course waiting for or assuming that there is a Father figure who will tell you what the law is, the belief that somebody on the planet knows what's going on and will sort it out for us if we are nice people and [unclear - we pay them enough-?] Anyway any group of people believes that somehow or other someone knows what is going on and somebody has the power to solve problems and so on and I have seen it happen in commercial organizations [unclear] it is the world in we believe that there are experts who actually know something more than other people, it is the world in which you believe that there are saints [unclear - and you can go and sit at their feet and get transformed -?] all of that is to with salvation [unclear] here we are and we are such poor, inadequate people but somewhere there is the light which can maybe come in and save us from ourselves.

Now this other form of revelation is using language in very sort of it is saying that 'No, in this politics eliminate this', and it doesn't mean that there isn't a God or there aren't angels or whatever it is you like to believe in but it has a practical difference and that is summed up for me in the famous phrase [from an American song -?], 'There's nobody here but us chickens'. In other word sitting in a group of people [long unclear] and occasionally the group will actually admit to each other, no they don't actually know what is going on and we both face up to that as being our situation. And what do we do? Well we respect what it is that we can actually see. [unclear] the tiny bit of light that each person in the group can offer is taken to be the [unclear] we are together for a reason to be with ourselves as we are and so what comes from this [unclear] revelation in the sense of here is the word of God on tablets brought from Mount Sinai but painfully fragmentally there is piece of [unclear]. Usually in the group of group process these smaller and emergent insights are dismissed, rejected, censored or treated as heretical or deviant and so on and so on. They are censored or reduced and they never actually play a role or a very little role in the behaviour of the group.

I said this is polemical because it tries to sharply divide two differing attributes it is like saying 'the cavalry, it will never come over the hill' you know, never, never, never, [unclear - we are mortal... drop dead and that's it! -?] Meanwhile while we are what can we say to each other? [unclear - As we are because only we can save each other -?]

Now the prospects of these two makes a challenge to what should be the standard in following of any spiritual teaching which is reliance on or belief in some system or teacher or a tradition which is supposed to embody the [unclear] truth and in which there is an investment and projection of [unclear].

This group, the one of revelation is in itself not denying anything. It is saying in terms of what we can do working together we have to deal with what we can produce for ourselves, we are the people in these specific conditions and only we can know what specifically what is appropriate and relevant to these conditions.

[Long unclear] ... the work starts exactly where a man is in life. [unclear]

And it has to do with the revelation of what this life is and it is quite different from the attitude of presuming that what this life is "being asleep "being mechanical", "many 'I's" or any such description by starting afresh.

One of the features of distinguishing these two [unclear] towards [unclear] the way of salvation you are in the group you look out, out here [unclear] and this is always labelled One. A unity. A lot of people think there is [unclear] a oneness in which all these other, if you could get all of us, these other people to agree then alright you can then follow this same oneness, and that would solve all our problems. But in this, whatever oneness there is not going to descend in us like a fairy godmother but it is going to be very pragmatic dealing with the real difference and diversity between us and that this very difference and diversity between us is the working fuel of any work group and is the fuel, it not like the [unclear] treating the group like a mechanism. [unclear] ... this means diversity of unity, unity is not monolithic is not one-valued, not of one colour, not of one belief, unity as in the original Greek word [Ptolemy] [unclear] the verse means turning, this means turning into the One, the universe is not that which exists as one but which is 'turning into the One'. So at any moment any group of people they can 'turn into the One' and this is not by silencing the scent or everywhere getting people to think the same thing. It is by building on the very diversity. [unclear].

[Long spell of interference on tape - reference to how little is known at all about how groups work/operate -?] And I think the conclusion was that in terms of in the realm of what is called the fourth way hardly anything was known [unclear] in Gurdjieff's description [unclear] you just hope that you have in your group someone everybody accepts as the leader or the teacher, [unclear] and this is just the same as any other institution, hierarchical, at best paternalistic which depends upon a Hierarchy in which the people at the top prevent information from reaching the people below and all that sort of thing. This is the way things are run in business corporations, in governments it is the way things are run in spiritual organizations. I had a friend who attended some years ago the Chicago Conference, a broad conference of religions and he looked [unclear] very carefully at the two hundred spiritual leaders at [unclear] and each one had a little block, a little enclave which protected them from any kind of real interaction or dialogue [unclear] So here they were gathered together at [unclear] conference and he said, like in any conference which happens at nearly every conference in the world before the conference starts they have a list of those propositions they are going to sign up to, which is sort of worked out beforehand and they all end up signing it at the end. [unclear] But nothing at all happens in a conference. And it is designed that way in order to perpetuate [unclear].

[Long unclear]

And I mention about the lack of knowledge about the group process because there is a prospect, and it very much intrigues me, and Karen as well, that when groups meet together there is a chance for another kind of mind to evolve which is, you can't really call it a group mind, and it is not a kind of a composite out of the people there it is a genuine independent phenomenon.

So not only to mix up languages, you have such things as mechanicality, falling asleep and fragmentation on an individual level you also have it in a group. [unclear] The kinds of group mechanisms that will prevail everywhere will prevail. [unclear] Unconscious projections, delusions and the sorts of modelings, emotional modelings, [unclear] I know for a fact that any of us can be aware can become aware of these processes happening.

[Long unclear - the fallacy of autonomy?]

This picture of autonomy is a fabrication of the last two thousand years it has very deep roots in the great religions such as Christianity and the dissemination of the idea that [unclear] one has of an immortal soul, an extraordinarily revolutionary concept but it has meant it has produced in our time this absolute madness and chaos of a world in which six billion people each one of which believes it has a mind and is an independent unit. Imagine! The situation of six billion autonomous units all believing that they are the centre of the universe. Quite staggering!

And so these questions are not only academic but have a bearing on all sorts of things such as the incredible, incredibly long-term going on sagas of ethnic conflict and other kinds of conflict going on in the world and now we come another aspect of all this.

Firstly, it irritates me when [unclear]… ancient wisdom neglecting certain, very telling teachers for good or ill which have come our way in the last few hundred years amongst which there really can't be concrete evidence that we lived on one planet. I say this and you say of course we live on one planet, you don't know how recent this is. Only the last one hundred years at most and then in the 1960's when Stuart [Randall?] [unclear] published that picture of the Earth from space one of the most revolutionary acts in the whole of human history. The whole world could see the Earth as a whole. You had great figures like Buckminster Fuller talking about providing a manual for space-ship earth. [unclear] His themes? Started about the same time as Gurdjieff and Gurdjieff was also part of the Zeitgeist. [unclear]

And relies on 'My God! This is a system! [unclear] There is one planet and there you see it ocean, atmosphere and rocks all permeated with life. Then as some of you know many of these ideas that Gurdjieff puts forward about the biosphere in his teaching were quite common among the Russian intelligentsia at the time including the remarkable man who the key man in fact who propagated the idea of the biosphere that is Vladimir Vernadsky.

And one of the two key people who propagated also the idea of the [unclear].

It is, the awareness of the life as a cosmic phenomenon was a very Russian thing in the 1920s. It wasn't just Gurdjieff. It is all part of this becoming aware for the first time of One Earth which is a system and there is no evidence that I know of any of the previous generations really having that knowledge. And it is absolute revolutionary knowledge, as well as the knowledge that the largest mass of living matter on this planet is microbial, it is not in insects, not in animals, not in fish, not in plants it is in microscopic life which was only known about around 150 years ago. The actual key component in the whole regulation of life is the microbial-system and 150 years ago we knew nothing about it!

I am confronted with a world and which very radically different and part of this planetary awareness is that for the first time the ordinary population of the world has to face this incredible revolution which is that there are other people on the planet who are also human. And you can see this is [unclear] but every traditional society treats itself as the humans and the other people as the not-so-human. For the first time everybody has to face the mystery of other people who are human as well. Absolutely mind-blowing. And it means that all the cultures of the world which we are [unclear] existence must be brought together and treated as part of one story.

Gurdjieff was an important pioneer too. I mention the coming together of cultures because it means the coming together of different views that we have. Remember in All and Everything a Beelzebub says, or a character says 'never will there be just one religion on earth' [unclear].

What is Mind? Seeing mind not just as the product of brains that contemporary scientists are dealing with but minds that are very cultural/social group process. That's, very I mean I just realize we just didn't have to deal with this [unclear] before. Inner [unclear] inner language, inner police system you had they the authorities [unclear] and then you had the thought police of the particular culture, and its true, Asian culture, Western culture both [had their] thought police and we more or less managed to get along. Now because they are [unclear] one against the other there is incredible friction it's like a model of buffers [unclear].

I think it's an area which needs to be addressed and it has a bearing how do I come to think and believe as I do?

What can I do about freeing myself from my conditioning?

How can people live genuinely beginning to think together?

Increasingly for me and some of my friends it doesn't matter what particular idea you happen to believe in at all. It is like; can it have become a gigantic supermarket of ideation? You can pick up material if you have time and money. You can pick up material from Stone-age cultures, from Asian cultures, Eskimo culture, Egyptian, African whatever you like you can go out with a shopping list. You can become a shaman you can meditate you can do Tantric Yoga and its wonderful you can go and shop amongst [unclear] you can believe whatever you like and it is like the whole pool is there, turned into a supermarket. And here is the other component which interests me. This hope or trail of the esoteric' need to be reinvestigated and one nice definition I came across, I think it was Aristotle, and he said a definition of 'the esoteric is that which is known for a long time but not understood'.

The naive idea that the esoteric is some box of knowledge which you can be privy too if you go through some special things does seem rather a restricted view. [unclear] There was a time of course in the last thousand years or so of European history when [unclear] alternative thoughts to those currently in societies were dangerous as a rule therefore people had to be protect them, you know the Freemasons the alchemists, Knights Templar all kinds of secrecy and codes and all the rest of it. But this inheritance of that way of dealing with the esoteric had [unclear] and this I believe no longer to be an appropriate model to follow. [unclear] protect themselves mainly by the sole recourse, and also Gurdjieff also pointed out, that most people don't want to know anyway. It is [unclear] freely available and nobody wants to know. So what was called the esoteric some time ago and the exoteric [unclear] it really isn't a special branch of knowledge, it is just knowledge.

[Unclear. Tape then quite inaudible.]

© Copyright 2001 – Antony Blake - All Rights Reserved

Higher Being Bodies: Their Origins and Functioning

H.J. Sharp

G. I. Gurdjieff told us that it was important that we believed nothing and trusted nobody. We therefore need to question everything in his published material and make comparisons with present day science and technology, questioning that also. Such questioning must above all be directed at any consideration of the origin and functioning of Higher Being Bodies.

Sy and Nicolas in their paper to follow will deal in detail with what Gurdjieff told us about Higher Being Bodies. In this presentation, I will simply try and indicate what really modern science tells about their possible origin and functioning. In the dialogue which has emerged through email over the last year the impression seems to have arisen that I did not indicate what we have to do of ourselves. I took it that our actions had nothing to do with the hardware. I fully concede that to become conscious in a Higher Being Body, we have to apply voluntary labour and conscious suffering in our relationship to others. I deliberately say "to be conscious in a Higher Being Body" because Gurdjieff told us that they are already present and functioning.

Put simply, based on those parts of modern science which seem very likely to be correct, it has taken some 3,000,000,000 years for organic life to evolve to the level of us humans, three brained sentient beings. The first 1,000,000,000 years were taken up solely with non-nucleate cells which significantly changed the Earth's atmosphere making it more suitable for multicellular organism and the arrival of the nucleate cells on which we are based. Then primitive bacteria which had within them self replicating molecules of much greater complexity than those in the non-nucleate cells, invaded them to give the first nucleate cells, a binary symbiotic organism. It then took a further 2,000,000,000 years for organic life to evolve to the level of the three brained human. For us humans to evolve further, to achieve a psychological evolution of significance, will take a further 1,000,000,000 years or so. The probability is that within this time span a major disaster will happen to the Earth such as will eliminate it and all on it. It would therefore seem to me essential that we as individuals do all that are possible to achieve such a psychological evolution in our individual life span. The overall effect of a significant number of humans achieving this is beyond us as we are.

To quote Maurice Nicoll: "Man is born with a great part of his brain unused, a fact which no mechanical theory of evolution by selection and immediate advantage can explain. These unused parts of the brain represent his further possibilities of individual evolution".[1]

---

[1] Maurice Nicoll. *The Commentaries*. Volume 1. Page 245.

2. Evidence for the Presence of an Entity of Higher Intelligence in the Personal Unconscious

The evidence for the influence of the personal unconscious and the collective unconscious is based upon many examples of "channelling" and the solution of problems by individuals while in dream or other special states and which the personal conscious mind had addressed for a prolonged period of time and failed to find a satisfactory solution. Cryptomnesia is another phenomenon now well established and which confirms the influences of an entity other than the personal conscious mind.

Cryptomnesia

For Frederick Myers, in contradistinction to his contemporaries such as Freud and Janet, the unconscious, or as he termed it, the subliminal - the secondary personalities revealed in trance states, dreaming, crystal gazing, and automatic writing - potentially possessed a higher intelligence than ones waking or supraliminal personality and often served to convey messages of guidance. Myers" work in this field paved the way for Theodore Flournoy.

Probably the most significant advance was made by Flournoy. This was in 1899, when he published "From India to the Planet Mars".[2] This was the result of investigations on a spiritualist medium who exhibited multiple personalities and "speaking in tongues". Flournoy's analysis and conclusions from his investigations laid the foundations for the present day ideas on the significance of the personal and collective unconscious. They would appear to be the reservoir of the total wisdom of humanity. One of the significant findings of Flournoy's investigations was that virtually all the material produced by the medium is based upon forgotten memories, which have been in some way recombined at an -unconscious level so as to be then injected into consciousness as an apparently original experience or information. Since Flournoy's work, however, explained the abilities of good mediums and clairvoyants, popular at the time, as being the result not of the spirits of the dead, but rather that of a higher entity within the individual, his work had a very mixed reception, eventually being in effect ignored and forgotten for a long period. It was eventually taken up by Jung who did acknowledge it as the origin of the concept of the personal and collective unconscious, although this was not until 1902-5.

There are many references to Cryptomnesia in Jung's Complete Works and these have been listed under the next reference.[3]

---

[2] Theodore Flournoy. *From India to the Planet Mars*. First published 1899. Reprinted by Princeton University Press 1994.

[3] C. G. Jung. *Complete Works*. Volume 1. Para 138-48. Volume 4. Para 152. Volume 5. Para 474, 68/2n. Volume 6. Para 839. Volume 7. Para 219. Volume 8. Para 311, 319, 503, 599, 845. Volume 9. Para 92, 549n. Volume 13. Para 352n. Volume 17. Para 200. Volume 18. Para 26, 454, 457. Volume 1. Para 166-186. Volume 6. Para 839n. Definition of: Volume 1. Para 180. Enrichment of conscious memories. Volume 1. Para 146.

So if we could become conscious of this higher intelligence already functioning in our unconscious, would this mean that we had developed a Higher Being Body?

Morton Schatzman

Morton Schatzman, an American psychiatrist, at the time based in London, in 1983, writing in the New Scientist[4], invited the readers to consider a number of brain-twisters and see if they could come up with a solution in their dreams. One of the puzzles was based on a sentence: "I am not very happy acting pleased whenever prominent scientists over magnify intellectual enlightenment". More than 200 readers responded giving a mass of evidence of the peculiar wisdom there is to be had from our dreams, in other words from at least our personal unconscious. Hence the old adage, "If you have a problem, sleep on it!"

A number of results from this experiment were subsequently reported by Peter Martin.[5] Roy Norvill also reports and comments on some of this material.[6]

A sixth form pupil who took part in the experiment had the following dream: I am giving a lecture to a number of scientists seated at round tables scattered about a large hall. Nobody is listening to me. This makes me very angry and I shout "I am not very happy!" The scientists seated at the tables nearest to me look up. Now awake, the pupil recalls the dream:

"It suddenly struck me that the scientists who had responded to me were seated at five separate tables - with one scientist at the table nearest to me, two at another table, three at a third table, and so on up to five. I began to feel that the numbers were important, and I counted the number of words in the sentence. As I did, I realised that it was the number of letters in each word that represented the answer. I counted the letters and arrived at the sequence 1, 2, 3, 4, 5, - - - 13. We should note also that when he shouts "I am not very happy! ", again we have the sequence 1, 2, 3, 4, 5!

All the other people who dreamed the correct answer to this problem had had dreams involving counting, one woman dreaming of a "Count"!

So in these examples, we have evidence of the workings of the personal unconscious mind and indications of its higher level of intelligence. Evidence, I would suggest of the importance of bringing together the personal conscious and unconscious minds so that they work truly as a symbiosis just as the basis of the hardware, the human body and mentation equipment is based on the symbiosis of the original non-nucleate cell and the bacterial organism which invaded it to form the first symbiotic organism all those many millions of years ago.

---

[4] Schatzman. Solve Your Problems in Your Sleep. New Scientist. 9th June, 1983.
[5] Peter Martin. "All you have to do is dream", YOU. 1983.
[6] Roy Norvill. *The Language of the Gods*. Ashgrove Press. 1987. Page 178.

Higher Being Bodies: Their Origins and Functioning

3. Other Examples of the working of a higher unconscious intelligence

To quote very briefly, we have Kekule von Stradonitz who in 1866 came to the understanding of the structure of the benzene ring as a result of a dream. This laid the foundations of modern organic chemistry. Jules-Henri Poincare is another who developed the idea of automorphic functions when not in a truly conscious state.

Then we have Mohammed who dictated the Koran when in some sort of trance state in which the Angel Gabriel visited him and gave him the teaching. On a number of occasions, however, some days after a particular message had in effect been channelled by him, he realised that this had not been the Angel Gabriel, but some other entity who had visited him. These are now known as the Satanic Verses.

So was Mohammed influenced by some greater mind, some entity beyond himself or was he simply influenced by material in his personal; unconscious? An important clue is given by the fact that he was an epileptic. One generally thinks of epileptics as people subject from time to time to major seizures involving spasmodic and uncontrollable movements of the musculature of the body. This is only one form, however, the grand mal form. But there is also the petit mal form with which there is no external indication of a seizure. They at most merely appear to be in a trance state.

4. Epilepsy

The typical grand mal epileptic seizure starts because a tiny cluster of neurones somewhere in the brain start misbehaving, firing chaotically, such activity spreading like wildfire. However it is extremely local; focused on a small patch of the brain. If such local seizures are in the motor cortex, the result is a sequential muscle twitching; they are called Jacksonian seizures. If the focus is in the limbic system, however, particularly in the region of the left temporal lobe, the result is an enhancement of emotion. In particular, there are feelings of enlightenment, of certainty, a feeling of a divine presence, a reality greater than ordinary reality. More than this, the evidence now is that the repeated passage of massive volleys of nerve impulses within the limbic system, permanently facilitates particular pathways and opens up new ones. In this way the mentation of the person is permanently changed and enhanced.

While many epileptic seizures result in brain damage and tragic long term consequences for the individual concerned, there is now evidence that in some cases, neuron storms in specific local areas of the frontal lobes produce permanently altered mental states. These may not relate to typical grand mal or petit mal seizures, but to similar extremely local hyper neuron activity.

It could well be that such local hyper neuron storms were what happened to Mohammed, and also to Abraham, to Moses, to Paul on the road to Damascus, to Jacob when he wrestled with the Angel and when he fell asleep and had the vision of Jacob's Ladder. All these special experiences of these people were characterised by a sense of utter conviction, more real than real, and a light that was both within and without. This is typical of frontal lobe hyperactivity, precipitated by something similar to petit mal seizures and leading to a permanent alteration in mentation abilities. This is surely a likely route to the creation of or conscious awareness of a Higher Being Body, the possession of which enables the human so endowed to operate at a higher level of mentation, understanding and experience.

5. The Reappraisal of Understanding in the Light of New Knowledge

There are many incredible journeys undertaken by some species of animals as part of their reproductive activity. The green turtles which normally live in the South Atlantic close to the shores of South America swim all the way across the South Atlantic to the shores of Africa where they make landfall on particular sandy beaches to lay their eggs. There are many examples of this sort of behaviour which makes no sense unless we go a long way back into history. One hundred million years ago only a narrow strip of sea separated the continents of South America and Africa. Plate tectonics has now changed all this resulting in the massive ocean separating them. The turtles traditional feeding ground was near the South American shore and they migrated to their traditional breeding ground of a sandy beach of an island a little off the coast. As the continents drifted apart, the turtles gradually swam a little further and further east, unable to consciously re-program their overall behaviour patterns.

It is only when we are able to relate the turtles behaviour to Plate Tectonics that it makes any sense. There are many examples where it would be useful to re-appraise conclusions of the past in the light of more recent knowledge.

While it may still be that individual neurons in the brain are not replaced when they die, there are so many of them, and the brain is now known to function on a complex hierarchical structure with multi pathways of any given function, that the brain function may go on increasing in sophistication through life. The evidence is that such further developments in mentation capability are not by means of the part of the brain concerned with moving or intellect, but rather the feeling function. In effect there is now concrete evidence for the possible development in certain individuals of a Higher Emotional Mind. This is in effect what Gurdjieff taught.

One of the most modern approaches to the origin of consciousness is dependent upon a practical understanding of the consequences of increasing distances between external information receptors and the developing central processing unit, the brain.[7]

The earliest sensors were an integral part of the cell membrane or the specialised skin surface of the early multicellular organisms. The sensor, when activated, was locally reactive. It is of interest that the neurological structures of the present human, develop in the foetus from the same germinal epithelium which also gives rise to the external skin and the lining layers of the alimentary canal.

---

[7] V. S. Ramachandran & Sandra Blakeslee. *Phantoms in the Brain*. Fourth Estate. London. 1999.

Higher Being Bodies: Their Origins and Functioning

The next stage of development was for the sensors to become more sophisticated and for the system to be based upon signals travelling to a more centrally placed ganglion and the response signal travelling from the ganglion to the peripheral areas needing to respond. In general these twin signals have a long distance to travel; dining which both the signals undergo attenuation. In any case the whole sequence is completed in a micro second. In the case of the typical unconditioned reflexes, such as the blinking of the eye; we generally have no conscious awareness that it has happened. Recent research based on the problems of phantom limbs, blind sight and so on, now indicates that there is now a secondary target for many of these responses and these take the form of a map of the whole physical body, spread over the superficial areas of the brain. So in many cases, in addition to the automatic response to the peripheral organs of reaction, there is another signal directed to the corresponding area of the map in the brain. The pathway for this signal is considerably shorter, and it in turn elicits a response on arrival at the relevant point on the brain surface map, thus producing an input signal to the original area of the brain. In this way a succession of signals, inputs and responses, it set up. Because the pathway is short, the diverted outgoing and new incoming sensory loops allow a stronger feed back effect; the original single signal from the peripheral receptor is followed immediately by a repeating signal of the short feed back loop. There is the minimum of attenuation and so the pairs of signals take time to degrade, it is this passing time span which gives us the feeling of awareness. In this way we live in a "Life Simulator" and it is this "Life Simulator" that we are conscious of, have awareness of not the "real" interaction of the surface of our physical body and our external environment. So here we have an explanation of the arrival of consciousness. This concept is dealt with in considerable detail by Nicolas Humphrey.[8] But there is more. Dependent upon the strength of the feed back loop signal, the degree to which it is energised to give increased amplitude, the experience can have a varying level of so called "reality". So perhaps we can see that if in some way we can inject extra or "higher" energies into the system, we will have an experience of greater intensity, sometimes "more real than real". In other words "Self Remembered" experiences which some of us do have at times. Similarly the experience of passing time can be varied. As the signal energy and/or frequency is increased, compared to an ordinary experience, the special experience has a different time value. In this way it could be possible to experience ordinary reality in the usual passing time, while at the same time or occasion to be conscious of an inner separate experience proceeding in another time, a time which in effect is faster than normal so that the concurrent normal reality appears to go slower than usual. Some of us have had such double reality experiences. Confirmation of all this in my view is given by our usual experience of unconditioned reflexes. Unless we make a special effort, the automatic blinking of the eye, for example, goes unnoticed by our consciousness; view is given by our usual experience of unconditioned reflexes. Unless we make a special effort, the automatic blinking of the eye, for example, goes unnoticed by our consciousness, since it is based on a single response. There is therefore insufficient duration of time for our conscious awareness.

---

[8] N. Humphrey. *History of Mind: Evolution and the Birth of Consciousness*. Harper & Collins, New York, 1993.

In conclusion I would suggest that we now have at least three areas for further investigation which may relate to the creation of Higher Being Bodies; the controlled production of small fire storms in certain frontal lobe areas, the additional energizing of the feed back loops which give rise to ordinary consciousness, and other means of encouraging the rearranging of neuron connections to give higher level circuitry.

And finally if there is a little time left to me I would like to give you all an example of being conscious in Higher Mind.

The "Presence"

So what has happened to the various Angels with which we started this and which played a special part at times. I have had no contact with them for some time now, although an Angel does make itself felt occasionally. The last time was in late 2000.

We were coming to the end of the day, on Sunday evening, October the 3rd, 2000. I had told my wife that I would shortly make her some Ovaltine that we would look at some of the BBC2 News and then take our time and go to bed. It was 10.30 in the evening.

I went to my little bar in the corner of the room and began to pour myself a drink as a night cap. I was present and fully aware of the me that was holding the bottle and carefully pouring, and then I was also aware, inside so to speak of a symbolic Angel. It was as if the Angel opened a door of access and a "Presence" poured in. The feeling was of something benign. There was no feeling of fear as I continued to watch the two realities. The inner one seemed to have a different time. In fact I began to realise that it was not in time and space. With it or as part of it came overwhelming feelings of a total embracing, of reassuring, and of a readiness to help when needed and accepted. I knew directly that I was sustained by it.

And with these feelings came an absolute knowledge, a direct knowing that all was so arranged from the beginning that when we individuals are ready, we could of ourselves, create the Higher level functioning of Heaven on Earth. Heaven as we call it exists in the world of ideas, beyond manifestation, and the wonder of the Godhead is that it has not created it, but is cultivating us in our own time so that we create it ourselves. The direct knowledge came that all possibilities exist out of time and space and so there is all we need to create what we are aligned to when we are ready and able. But we have first to complete our own creation so that we are in proper order and correctly functioning.

So reality is a priceless gift, given us by the Godhead together with all we need to become, to create God. We are in the image of the Godhead. We are part of the totality. The paradox is that we are the creators of the priceless gift that we have been given.

And then I noticed that I had finished pouring my drink in the few seconds which had passed and the Angel had disappeared as the vision which had lasted an eternity concluded. I must try and put it down in words, but I know the words will be totally inadequate.

© Copyright 2001 – H. J. Sharp - All Rights Reserved

On Higher Being-Bodies: The Gurdjieffian View

Nicolas Tereshchenko and Seymour Ginsburg

Recently expressed views that the crystallization of the "higher being bodies" in a "three-brained/centred" being can come about simply through certain organic conditions such as epilepsy are not accordance with our understanding of the Gurdjieffian teaching. We are convinced that Gurdjieff's teaching insists that "being-Partkdolg-duty", defined as "conscious labors" and "intentional suffering", is necessary for the coating and perfecting of the "higher being-bodies". It is clearly stated in *Beelzebub's Tales to His Grandson* that:

"owing to just those factors which our COMMON FATHER CREATOR ENDLESSNESS consented to foreordain to be the means by which certain of the Tetartocosmoses - as a final result of their serving the purposes of the common-cosmic Iraniranumange - might become helpers in the ruling of the enlarged World and which factors also until now serve as the sole possible means for the assimilation of cosmic substances required for the coating and perfecting of the higher being-bodies and which we at the present time call 'conscious labors' and intentional suffering.'"[1]

According to the information in *Beelzebub's Tales to His Grandson*, only "three-brained" or "three-centred" beings can have "higher being-bodies". This includes the Keschapmartnian three-brained Tetartocosmoses living on the planet Earth that is us, men and women.

Additionally, Gurdjieff's teaching points to the necessity of the proper use of the essential substance Exioehary, the highly refined energy produced in the sexual organs, for the coating of the "higher being-bodies". The proper use of this substance, other than for procreation, is spoken about in every esoteric tradition. About Exioehary, Gurdjieff in *Beelzebub's Tales* says:

"this sacred substance arises in the presences of all beings without distinction of brain system and exterior coating, chiefly in order that by its means they might, consciously or automatically, fulfil that part of their-being-duty which consists in the continuation of their species; but in the presences of three-brained beings it arises also in order that it might be consciously transformed in their common presences for coating their highest being-bodies for their own being."[2]

---

[1] Gurdjieff, G.I. *All and Everything, First Series: Beelzebub's Tales to His Grandson* (New York: Harcourt, Brace & Co., 1950), 792.
[2] Gurdjieff, *Beelzebub's Tales to His Grandson,* 1950 *ed.,* 276.

Higher Being Bodies: The Gurdjieffian View

Gurdjieff tells us about the most ideal and perfect of all the "three-brained/centred" Triakrkomnian beings in the universe which are those arising on the incomparable and marvellous planet Modiktheo.

Of them he says, "At their very arising they already have all the being-bodies" (*Beelzebub's Tales*, 773). However, this possibility is denied "three-brained/centred" beings arising on all other planets for whom the sole possible means of assimilating the necessary cosmic substances for coating of the "higher being-bodies" are "conscious labours" and "intentional suffering" (*Beelzebub's Tales*, 773,792).

The task of the assimilation of necessary cosmic substances for us "three-brained/centred" beings on planet Earth is made even more difficult than for "three-brained/centred" beings of other planets, because through heredity we are affected by the crystallized consequences of the organ Kundabuffer. These consequences, including the premature destruction by us of other beings on our planet, have caused a lessening of the number of sources for the emanation of the vibrations that great nature requires of us. Consequently, she has been compelled to actualize our presences under the principle of "Itoklanoz" (normally applicable only to "one-brained" and "two-brained" beings) rather than the "Foolasnitamnian" principle that is proper to the existence of all "three-brained/centered" beings on any planet of our great universe. This alteration in the actualizing of our presences has resulted in our much shortened life span and accordingly gives us much less time than "three-brained/centered" beings on other planets for assimilating the necessary cosmic substances for coating of the higher being-bodies" (*Beelzebub's Tales*, 130-132).

Therefore, to form "higher being-bodies" we must work, and work very hard and persistently. For us, in order to grow, or "coat" as Beelzebub calls it, these additional vehicles (or bodies), it is necessary to unceasingly practice "being-Partkdolg-duty", defined as "conscious labors" and "intentional suffering" (*Beelzebub's Tales*, 792), within the limited life span given to us. These bodies never form automatically or UNconsciously, only through conscious work-on-self.

Related to this and not to be overlooked is Beelzebub's relating to Hassein of the text of the decree placed by our Common Father over the chief entrance of the holy planet Purgatory. It is that planet to which beings, who have coated their higher being-bodies, are merited to dwell. That decree states, "Only He May Enter Here Who Puts Himself In The Position Of The Other Results Of My Labors" (*Beelzebub's Tales*, 1164).

Additionally, let us not overlook the aforementioned essential substance, Exioehary, produced by the human three-story factory from the "first being-food", which must be present as the physical structure from which these "higher being-bodies" are built.

In researching the Gurdjieffian view on this subject; our attention was drawn to an earlier edition of *Beelzebub's Tales to His Grandson*, which we wish to bring to the attention of the conference. This earlier edition, we are informed, was produced by the book committee of the New York group under the guidance of A. R Orage, and privately published in 1931.

J. G. Bennett recounts the history of this earlier edition:

"When Gurdjieff returned to Europe in 1930 after the break-up of the old Orage groups, there was a very small sum left in the treasury to be used for any purposes connected with his work. Paul Anderson, who was then treasurer, worked out a proposal for producing a mimeographed edition of *Beelzebub* from the chapters Gurdjieff had left with them. The funds available were just enough to pay for the editing, proof-reading and printing of 102 copies, but not for binding. Two were reserved for Paul and Naomi Anderson who had done all the work and the remainder were sold at prices varying from $10 to $100 according to what pupils could afford.

"The version of *Beelzebub's Tales* that was published at that time is of great interest. It is in some ways easier to understand than the final version, published in 1950, and the French translation, published a few years later. The greatest changes were made in the chapter 'Purgatory'. He also changed some of the 'keywords', particularly the words describing the two fundamental laws... But, of course, there is very much more to this revision than the new words. In particular, the old version is much more explicit of the stages in man's development, which become disguised in the later-version and are much harder for the reader to understand."[3]

This earlier edition, like the earlier edition of the work of any author, is often seen as having been improved upon by the author's later edition. In this respect, it can be argued that Gurdjieff's conclusive views on the various subjects dealt with appear in the 1950 edition, published shortly after his death. But because the 1931 edition was easier to understand, Bennett asks the question: "Why should Gurdjieff have made a chapter that was already difficult, even harder?"

Bennett gives this answer: "He himself (Gurdjieff) used to listen to chapters read aloud and if he found that key passages were taken too easily - and therefore almost inevitably too superficially - he would rewrite them in order, as he put it, to 'bury the dog deeper.'"[4]

We think, as Bennett and others have thought, that Gurdjieff intentionally rewrote sections of *Beelzebub's Tales* to make his meaning more opaque. For this reason, we believe that there is great value to the pupil of Gurdjieff's teaching to obtain and to study the earlier 1931 edition.

In the present instance, for example, it is clear to us that the proper use of Exioehary, produced from refinement of the first being food, is required for the coating of the "higher being-bodies". But in the 1950 edition we are told that "these sacred substances, Abrustdonis and Helkdonis are just those substances by which the higher being-bodies of three-brained beings, namely the body Kesdjan and the body of the Soul, are in general formed and perfected."[5]

---

[3] Bennett, J. G. *Gurdjieff: Making a New World* (New York: Harper & Row, 1973), 175-176.
[4] Bennett, 274.
[5] Gurdjieff, *Beelzebub's Tales to His Grandson,* 1950 ed., 1106.

Higher Being Bodies: The Gurdjieffian View

It is not at all clear from the wording of the 1950 edition, just what the substances Abrustdonis and Helkdonis are, nor is their relationship to Exioehary spelled out. But when we look at the 1931 edition, the matter becomes clearer:

The beings of the continent Atlantis called the second food 'Abrustdonis' (air) and the third 'Helkdonis' (impressions). Regarding these two foods as very important and the productive feeding on them as their most important duty, the evolution of substances of Exioehary in most of them began to proceed as it proceeds in almost all the three-centred beings on all the planets of our great Megalocosmos...

Going on to speak about the misunderstanding of abstinent monks about this matter, Gurdjieff continues:

"It naturally never enters the heads of these monks, that although it is possible to perfect oneself by means of Exioehary, yet this perfection can proceed only through the conscious consumption and digestion of the substances Abrustdonis and Helkdonis, and this is why of course, no effective result has ever been obtained from their abstinence, or will ever be obtained...

"And only the substances of-the Abrustdonis and Helkdonis can be of any assistance to the Exioehary. Without these substances, the substances of the Exioehary, having no possibility of evolving further, and at the same time being unable to remain in the transitory centre of gravity of the Law of Eftologodiksis (Heptaparaparshinokh in the 1950 edition) soon begin to involve in the machine bodies of these unfortunate monks."[6]

We have referred here to the 1931 edition of *Beelzebub's Tales* in addition to the 1950 edition in support of this view of the requirements for the coating of the higher being-bodies.

In our preliminary study of portions of the 1931 edition we have found much useful information and much that elucidates matters that appear unclear in the 1950 edition. For example, as well as a somewhat greater clarity on what the substances "Exioehary", "Abrustdonis" and "Helkdonis" are, the early-version contains a bombshell, which we believe also provides the solution to the mystery of the "Choot-God-litanical" period.

Here is what Gurdjieff suddenly tells us in the 1931 edition:

"At the present time, of those real souls, formed and perfected in those beings themselves, there are very few on the planets. They were formed only in the first beings formed directly of the Microcosmoses, and in the bodies of their true heirs. Thus all the real souls have long ago nearly perfected themselves. ... Nevertheless at the present time there are on nearly all the planets of the Universe very many beings with souls. But these souls are, let us say, souls of the second order.

---

[6] Gurdjieff, G. I. *Beelzebub's Tales to His Grandson* (New York: privately published, 1931).

Although similar to real souls, they were not formed in the manner I have just described; and they are formed for quite other reasons."[7]

It is our hope that pupils and scholars more closely examine this earlier edition of *Beelzebub's Tales to His Grandson* to better understand Mr. Gurdjieff's teaching.

© Copyright 2001 - Nicolas Tereshchenko and Seymour Ginsburg - All Rights Reserved

---

[7] Gurdjieff, G. I. *Beelzebub's Tales to His Grandson* (New York: privately published, 1931).

Higher Being Bodies: The Gurdjieffian View - Questions & Answers

Contribution 1: I would like to open this session, but I cannot be impartial in the ordinary sense.

Contribution 2: We are asking questions about the presentations. I would like to make a small question which could be a way of dealing with the enormous complexity of the topics in Bert and Sy's talks and in your comments. Because I think of maybe 10 items that seem initially most important mentioned in the talks. For me it would be interesting to know, and I would come back to what Keith said earlier. Keith suggested that the terminology or perhaps what Mr. Gurdjieff said had changed in some way as time passed. I don't know. The only thing that I know is that in the music and movements there was a definite relationship in that we did something else earlier and something else later. This could be treated as a digestion of his earlier material and a new form that he made later in his life. This is normal for a creative genius. So why not for his thinking. What brings me back to this, the lectures, and somebody else can say what they wish as a contribution. It was about Higher being Bodies and the way they are put into operation. Am I correct in this?

Contribution 3: I was trying to very briefly list the findings of really modern science, indicating the possibilities of the development of what I would call the hardware. I am probably incorrect, but one has to try and relate this to one's real experience. And I think that the message I am trying to put over is that there is now uncontroversial evidence for what is known as Cryptomnesia, that in each of us there is an unconscious part of us that has a higher intelligence, and which is nudging us, pointing us in a certain direction. At times there is information from the race, from the collective unconscious which is trying to get us into a state in which it can work through us. We are a tool. What interests me is that in Aristotle's *Ethics* it says that he did not approve of some of his pupils standing on a platform and spouting his ethics as if they were indulging in an ego trip. He said that was not what they were to be used for. They were to be applied for the benefit of society. So he called them by a Greek word Organon, which means a tool. And we use the same root word for organic life. So organic life is a tool to be used by something higher, to be used by it to serve its purpose, for the completion of what is intended. And this is why we have the responsibility of paying for our arising by completing ourselves in order to better serve the purpose of the higher. And this is what I can see clearly, Jesus riding into Jerusalem on an ass; the ass is the three lower aspects of mind, while Jesus is the higher emotional and higher intellectual or perhaps the already functioning Higher Being Bodies. All together it represents the God-Man, riding into Jerusalem which is the Hermetic code for entering Greater Mind. And this is why I am quite sure in my own mind that much of what Gurdjieff wrote later is in the Hermetic code. The three times he was shot is all simply laid out in *Life is Real Only Then, When "I am"*, as the three stages of the initiation process.

Contribution 4: My question is as follows. In the fragments the word Higher Being Bodies is not mentioned. He mentions Astral body and I get the impression from reading this chapter that the Astral body was a very rare thing, that very few people have it. That it was there, or that it was not at all, like water boiling, and that it could only be obtained through tremendous efforts. Now in *All & Everything*, it is not put in that way; at least I did not understand it that way. So there is a contradiction that can be very meaningful, because if I would have it in the sense given in the Fragments, like water that has to be boiled, I could control it and I could use it at will. But if I have it and its still cloudy, overshadowed by forces I do not control, it can speak only from time to time. Then the existence of these Higher Being Bodies in us would explain an enormous amount of unexplainable things like Angels and so on, having forces that are incomprehensible to us. I was very moved by you telling us of the Angel because I attach great value to that.

Contribution 5: There is a Sufi saying "Angels are the powers hidden in the organs and faculties of man".

Maybe Angels are symbols of transformation. I think that what you are saying highlights one of the problems we have when we use words. We must not be too hidden bound by the words. The same word means one thing to one person and another to another. I cannot quote where the teaching is, but it is based on asking the key question "What are you?" You are not your body; it is not the one you were born with. Your mother fed the one you were born with and then you have since fed it so now it is much larger, but it is not something you possess. You are not your clothes, you bought them. You are not your personality; you made that by copying others. So what are you? You are your essence, your soul. But that has to be fed with the food of impressions as your body has to be fed. But essence is normally smothered by personality which is too active. So personality has to be quietened so that you can use it instead of it using you. Essence can then begin to be fed and grow. This is when the Virgin birth of the Christian teaching occurs. Essence then begins to quicken and grow. You can call this a Higher Being Body. In this way your soul can grow and benefit from life experiences while at the same time serving as a tool for something higher.

Contribution 6: Yes, Gurdjieff means the same thing when he describes the Astral body in 1950 or he describes the Higher Being Body later.

Contribution 7: That was a term used by the Spiritualists during that earlier period, the Astral body.

Contribution 8: Gurdjieff used the term Kesdjan body and he does not talk about Higher Being Bodies at all. There is a distinction between the Body Kesdjan and the Spiritual Body. He talks about air as in some way being the substance of the Body Kesdjan where as impressions are mentioned as the substance of the Spiritual Body.

Contribution 9: But it seems to be put in a much milder and broader context in his later writings.

Higher Being Bodies: The Gurdjieffian View - Questions & Answers

Contribution 10: As I recall it he notes four bodies and the bodies are presented apart from higher entities and I cannot be certain of what the relationship was between the bodies and the higher centres. And I know that there are places in *In Search* where he raises the question of epilepsy as a trigger for a pathological connection to a Higher Center. He describes all the various states that indicate that they had momentary connection to a higher center. But he describes them as pathological. But I have not seen any description of higher centres in *Beelzebub's Tales*. They are bodies, but there is no fundamental logical, unmetaphorical term for centres.

Contribution 11: I found it helpful to clearly distinguish just for the purposes of clarity between feelings and emotions. I take it that feelings relate to the functioning of the ductless glands; I feel afraid, I feel hungry, I feel cold. I feel afraid because there is a surge of adrenaline. This is nothing to do with emotions. Emotion is at a higher level, beyond feelings, and this is why we get confused when we talk about the feeling part being involved in love. Feelings are never part of love, only like or dislike because the feeling part is ambivalent. But once one is in Higher Emotional state, one loves unconditionally. This is the Love of God which passes understanding, because it is beyond the intellectual mind. It is a higher level function. Orage has quite an interesting book which describes the three basic or principle forms of love. Instinctive love gives no problem. No one is owed, everyone is satisfied and it leads to the perpetuation of the race. Feeling love gives all the problems because one feels owed because the love is not exactly what the lover wanted. The third is conscious love which asks for nothing in return. it merely wants to be accepted. But this is very rare in us humans. it is related to the Higher Emotional mind. That is as I see it, but that is just me.

Contribution 12: I thought it was the contrary. Emotion every animal can have. It is expressed as love for children. Animals love their young just as we do. If I have a sexual desire, yes. If I hate someone I can have an adrenaline surge and so it is an animal emotion. If it comes with some chemical or not, it is that same.

Contribution 13: If we look at Paul D. MacLean's material, *The Triune Brain in Evolution*, the first brain is the Reptilian brain, an automatic system for attack or defence, no awareness. This first brain is represented in us by the spinal cord and base of the head brain. The second brain comes at the time of the dinosaurs. They had a bad press, but they were the first to exhibit care of the young, learning through play, audio-vocal communication. This second brain is represented in us by the limbic system and the ductless glands. The third one which arrived with Homo Sapiens is represented in us by the cerebral hemispheres. Then we have the possibility of higher mentation by using these three brains additively or even interactively. But again this is only words. I just happen to find it for me of use.

Contribution 14: The diagram of nutrition in Ouspensky's work where you see the octave of the physical body, the food evolution occurring in parallel and interactively the evolution of food, air and impressions. What we see as the physical body is the composite of those three bodies operating on each other and together. The impression octave does not start until point 6.

Contribution 15: Correct. The thinking part of the human octave does not start until point 3. Then you see if you take it all round until you get to point 9 you have three hydrogens 6. So you have 666.

What I have then done is to put the further evolution on a second enneagram which is the reverse of the first one, and on it are Higher Emotional and Higher Intellectual. it is a model that may be of use to some people but not to others.

Contribution 16: I'd like to make a distinction about feelings. Now feelings are all over my body. Every time I make a facial gesture or assume a posture or have certain gesticulators, that is my feelings manifesting in my body. My feelings don't have a language except expressed through the body. So one must do certain things in order for the body to be able to stand on its own feet. And as a result of that I make it grow from my feelings to my heart and my emotions stand on their own and I can begin to have an emotional language that does not have to be expressed through the physical body. It was quite clear to me yesterday during the demonstration. There was a deep emotional reception from this demonstration of the music. And that is quite distinct from my ordinary feelings which are purely mechanical and that is the reason why can sense the awakening of some other centre than the intellectual in the physical body which allows the body to stand on its own feet and participate in relevant centres which are separate and less connected, and from these I can make this grow towards my heart and substances which begin to occur after that can wash down and wash my heart and make it pure. To me the explanation is so simple as I can observe it in myself. I don't have to think about mathematical formulae. It is there and I observe it in myself during the demonstration. I feel it is quite separate from my ordinary feelings and it exists only in embryo and exists on a certain level in the octave and is available in most people but on different levels of the octave. And it is up to me to complete the octave through work on myself

Contribution 17: I wonder if Gurdjieff puts emphasis on our being third force blind. And one way of understanding that blindness seems to be emphasised by the function of emotions which have been almost completely atrophied. This interconnectedness that we make of events through triadic function seems to have failed. It would seem that our first and very long struggle is to become reconnected to our ordinary emotional centre. Many people in ordinary life assume they already have that connection. Gurdjieff said we do not. So maybe much of what we talk about in words that we put in the category of higher emotional centre really has to do with the centre we are not connected to, our ordinary emotional centre. We are not three brained beings, but peculiar three brained beings. Peculiar because we have lost this contact with the Holy Reconciling which is our feelings, all part of emotions. So perhaps we have to emphasise that we have to struggle to become reconnected inside of us in ordinary life so that we are really normal three brained beings and have a real emotional centre that functions in every single event, before we get to defining the subjective nature of Higher Emotional Centre which is something quite different, once we have a normal emotional centre.

Contribution 18: You can try and make that connection by an act of will. I don't know if this helps, but if you consider the concepts of Kundalini Yoga and the chakras, we have a familiar pattern of relationships. The chakras are considered vortices of energy situated in ascending order along an invisible spinal nerve, the shushumna. The lowest, the root chakras, instinctive-moving, is concerned with simple primal holding on to life necessary in infancy and childhood. The second, the svadhishthana, the genital chakra becomes hyperactive at puberty and corresponds to feeling. The third, the manipura of navel chakra is concerned with the will to power. This can be used positively as power and mastery achieved with pride and of constructive purpose for the benefit of all it can also be used negatively as an insatiable will to conquer and subjugate and own for oneself by the almost exclusive application of intellect alone. The development of the ordinary individual stops with the activation of these three lower chakras. If, however, the fourth chakra, the heart chakra, the anahata, becomes active it opens the heart to love. In addition it also makes available energies from higher chakras or centres, the visudda at the level of the larynx. This enables the functioning of the navel chakra to become only positive and creative. Later there is the ajna chakra at the level of the head and the sahasrara chakra, the lotus above the head.

Contribution 19: You spoke about the Virgin Birth. As I understood it, it is a change that takes place in some of us. We no longer see ourselves as physical body, personality and so on but as Endlessness manifesting through us. It seems to me that this is what this process is about. I just want to share what I heard Prof. Thring say. Somebody asked him about exercises and he said the exercise that was most meaningful to him was the one the Gurdjieff gave to Margaret Anderson. He said you can't do this but you need to try and that is to say "I am" every hour. And this is very practical and it seems that you talk about this as an act of will and there may be something like that which helps to bring about this change. I do not know if that is a crystallizing or formation of a Higher Being Body, but it seems to be in that direction.

Contribution 20: I pray every day and night and sometimes during the day, and I always start it off by trying to feel what it would be like if I had never been born. But I have been born into this life. What am I going to do with it? If I am not fully awake, fully aware, fully related to everything around me, I will waste what God has given me, so I pray that I do not waste a moment. So I must try to stay awake, try to be present for every moment. It is rather like being given two tickets for a special play at the theatre. So you go into the theatre with the tickets, but if you do not pay attention to the play every moment you will waste the tickets. So having been born into life, what are you going to do with it? Are you going to waste it?

Contribution 21: If I may come back. I am just trying to organize for myself what has been said. I feel it is my duty to make a sort of overview of what has been said. I don't know. Some things I have to think about. There are many things said that I have to think about maybe for quite a long time. That is useful. That is the use of such a Conference that you have something to comment upon. And from the other aspect we have to try to be perfected and productive. This haunting chapter of this Dervish living in an electric lighted cave doing experiments is amazing. An incredible chapter. And the only thing that I can come up with to explain the contradiction between what has been said at the Conference and this chapter is that when he describes the sheep or his dog that give higher quality vibrations than man, is because man is in his mental sphere, while the dog or the sheep are in their emotional sphere. So that the man who produces less energy or whatever on the little measuring machine. The mental man is on a lower level than the sheep. That is what he meant in my understanding. It is the mental that crushes the feeling and sensation. Therefore the voltage is lower. His capacity is much higher than the dog or the sheep, but he has destroyed his own possibility, or it may be the crystallized consequences of the organ Kundabuffer. But I would like to finish as follows. Now it is important that as a mechanism, I am convinced that feelings go on all the time in me, but could not be measured on the Dervish machine because of the crushing of the feelings. There is no doubt that it happens all the time to me. The emotions go on all the time but they cannot come to the machine of the Dervish. The machine of the Dervish represents for me consciousness of man. Consciousness. What he is aware of himself. Now if somebody brings the cookie here and I want to take the biggest one, but if my mind does not allow me to see that I am greedy for the biggest cookie, which as a matter of fact I am. But my mind does not allow me that because the mind's opinion about myself stops me taking the biggest one. But the emotion is there. The greed is there. Now somebody speaks. I hate him! Why I don't know. My mind suppresses that feeling. I hate him! That feeling goes on all the time but I am not aware of it. So the little machine of the Dervish cannot feel it. The consciousness of the dervish is not fed by what is going on. Now a large part of what I was taught in the early days was to be aware of what is actually going on in those centres by self observation. Because only if you know more or less what is going on in those enlightened moments when you actually see you are jealous of somebody else or - - all these stupid reactions. They are not stupid, they are there. As a matter of fact I am much more alive than my mental image of myself this is a construction of false personality. Now the question is the same as we put yesterday during our presentation. What are you going to do if you run out of energy or you need more energy. The little Dervish machine has to operate on a certain level; the dog has to bring its energy, from other centres. And what was said about feelings and emotions. But I would not know the answer to the difference between feeling and higher emotional. I would not know how to deal with that part. I know if I want energy I need honesty in my consciousness as to what I truly am.

Contribution 22: Sensation is something in my heart. It is just like when you sense your body. So you can also sense your heart at times. I practice opening my heart. It requires practice. It is not something that happens overnight. But that is the process. One must be able to get in touch with my heart. As Mr. Nyland says, if sometime I can do that, my heart can begin to sing. If my heart sings I am no longer in a mechanical way of doing things. And that is a definite tangible experience I can go through and I know where it is localised. It is not in my left foot, it's in my heart. And the expansion that takes place in my heart - I know that that has been awakened by the movement. I know that if I can love the planet and take care of it, I can put that kind of sensation in my heart. Then something can really happen, it is then an exercise in my heart. And if I do that constantly, then it becomes more and more awake. If I listen to certain music, it is almost like breaking an egg and all the substance pours out and enters my body. That is a definite experience. It is not an intellectual theory. For me, I want to know how to do that. I don't fear it. I must know how to do that. So you take what steps may enable you to do it. But I have to do it or it is only theory.

Contribution 23: This is the compulsion "I am".

Contribution 24: (unclear - Could not decipher this)

Contribution 25: This is something I want to tell you about emotional energy. You will all see why I am dubious about talking about this, but nevertheless there is a process of mental exercises you can go through that permits levitation. It is a series of mental exercises that produce an influx of energy like a vortex that raises you up. And measurements have been made of various physiological components such as brain waves and so on. This is what reassures me. During that first effects of stimulation all the brain waves are in synchronicity. Now what that means is a question. You make the measurements, then you observe the physical effects, then maybe you can come up with a theory.

Contribution 26: I think what Wim said about the mind squashing the body of emotion and what you say about the body which would indicate that the mind has not near as much capacity to squash the body. In *In Search* the body is presented in its parts as it moves from the lowest to the highest in one circumstance and from the higher to the lower in another. So perhaps that would indicate that the mind that Wim is speaking of is a mind that is associated with a certain part that is in the body, the moving part.

Contribution 27: The contradiction is where what you call "I". This I is a little bit of distance in the sense of trying to observe myself. And there is not a true contradiction. It is only if the life of the body and the life of the feelings are allowed to enter this observer. But the body of course is doing what it wants and the mind simply follows. But then you are as Harry indicates, this operating on that level. As you want to see and observe like the Dervish with his observation, his awareness of what is going on. I think that could solve the contradiction. Now for me also as regards this levitation, for me the most urgent thing is still practicing Movements. They are of tremendous help. Because you realise that so much is going on that you don't know. The observer wants to know, "May I be there?" To see what is going on. And the danger for me is that any action up to a higher world that denies the lower one would be a catastrophe. I agree with the necessity of a higher world being one, but it may never squash the feeling because then I would be alone out in the higher world and I cannot survive. It has cost me about 60 years to realize that I am a bridge. I must accept that I am. The higher world wants to go to my lower world, but I may not deny my feelings. Otherwise the higher force cannot come in.

Contribution 28: Yes, precisely. Except I would say I can have this witness as you call it. I wish for it all the time. It can only bear certain ideas. Later on as it grows up the wish does not have to be so strong. But it is there, this third system. But I must keep myself in practice in order for it to penetrate or to observe me. If all my feelings that are there and all my thoughts, hence the vibration it too dense - But for it to try and penetrate my thoughts and feelings it is like trying to listen to a Mozart string quartet in the middle of a steel mill. It just cannot do it.

[Rest of tape too distorted to transcribe.] End of Session

Seminar 5 - Oskiano

Facilitator: Nick Bryce

(Note from Nick: Every new paragraph indicates a change of speaker. No major editing changes have been made in this transcript. Sections which were unclear have been omitted. Much of the tape was inaudible.)

What "G" refers to as the mis-education of our youth. Oskiano that he speaks of here has a resonance to sensation picturings. In other words, a whole life experience is what feeds a 3-brained being. There must be something that can be good for the intellect and for the feelings. Anything less than that, when we try, for instance, to portion out as we do in modern education as simply fill up the mind with facts without a corresponding effort to have that resonate in our feeling centre and our sensory motor. The doing, the experience, in or to plant something inside of us. This seems to be one of the characteristics of *Meetings* when he is talking about education and not just for the sensory motor or just for the intellect.

In a wider sense I had a great deal of difficulty looking at this topic. So much of the book is involved with mis-education. What he calls the "Maleficent effects of the organ Kundabuffer" seems to permeate the entire humanity for eons. This is a huge, huge subject mis-education.

What impresses me about the book and the relationship that Beelzebub has with taking responsibility towards Hassein for his education is that he educates his grandson through his grandson's (innocence). What matters to him? And that would enable Hassein, or any of us, to engage the whole of ourselves.

Mr. G. tried to educate us, the reader, through movements or music, etc. because he knew he couldn't reach each of us in the same way. He understood that we were limited. But we have the capacity to feel and enjoy music.

If we are interested in something we have a greater capacity to hold our interest.

Does anyone think there is a relationship between Hassein's education and 'G's own education in the 2nd Series, where he goes to great lengths to describe his own education?

I see the relationship - how 'G' was educated as a youngster - his father told long stories and taught him in parables - which he in turn is trying to do for us.

As a very young child, 'G' was being coaxed to reason, as opposed to us today who learn by rote and not taught to reason.

One thing I've been wondering about in the last few months, non-related to *Beelzebub's Tales*, is how Beelzebub taught his grandson. There seems to be two pertinent elements: one is that he didn't give entertainment, and the other is that he allowed his own experience to flow by association of the time he spent in the solar system ORS. And he selectively chose what was relevant to Hassein's question in the moment. And often other things would come up. He had the discipline within himself to discriminate what was important now and what he could take up later. What I am wondering about is how that transformed Beelzebub himself over the course of the time he was educating his grandson. It seems to me that Beelzebub himself goes through a transformation and a real period of growth during the time in which he has chosen to educate his grandson. So it becomes a kind of mutual educational experience.

There was nothing childish about Beelzebub's education of Hassein. They discussed very weighty subjects. We don't do that with our children. We teach in a superficial way. Do you think children are capable of being able to absorb such material?

I want to go back to someone else's comment about interest. When I think back on 'G's education, it changed frequently. It did not seem to depend on what he was interested in. As soon as he was able to capture the essence of how to do something it was changed. Normal children, as soon as they become interested, they want to keep doing it and are disappointed when it's taken away from them. For 'G', his education seems to have been directed to a whole range of physical capacities. As regards the *Tales*, Hassein is entering puberty here. His intellectual part is about to open. Why is he interested? Does he start out as interested? He is curious. Beelzebub comments to Hassein that he is becoming more and more fond of these 3-brained beings. Terms like "your favorites" etc. become more frequent as the book goes on. But what was there to begin with? Curiosity? Why would Beelzebub choose to focus on that? How long does this education take over the time?

I think it's useful to look at your question. Why is Hassein interested in terms of us? Whilst you focused on young children as you see them. Oskiano has to do with his re-education of us. Curiosity perhaps is what brought us to the Work, or some kind of dissatisfaction. So here we are - we're Hassein. And he is going to destroy mercilessly everything in us about the way we existed. So this is a huge re-education.

The key thing I am hearing here is how 'G's father told him stories. Then the education of Hassein through stories. And again in Chapter 7, he felt he wasn't ready. Only when he was ready could he make those decisions. But the book isn't a book – it's a way of telling us a story. And that for me is the Oskiano.

All & Everything Conference 2001

I think it's too superficial to attach ourselves to the state of Hassein. Hassein has had a complete normal, balanced education. And he is ready at the age of 12 to take responsibility.

That doesn't seem very typical of us. We are mis-educated. That is why it is required to Destroy mercilessly. But this is not the case for Hassein. I haven't for a long time thought that the analogy to us really holds up. Beelzebub and Hassein are both from Paradise. They both have cosmic responsibilities.

What you say could be true but I still get the feeling that in all these Tales that he is talking to me. He is trying to destroy in me everything that's existing because it's all untrue.

About the age of 12 for a boy would be when the second totality's factors would start to change to bring in the third totality where objectivity has to be brought into play for true responsibility. To complete the preparation for a true responsible age. 'G' is perhaps indicating that we are at a stage really- because of our mis-education - only operating in the second totality, and Hassein is receiving the education we ought to receive.

Don't you think he is telling us how to raise our own kids?

I think he is telling us many things, both in the narrow sense and in the bigger sense.

In *Meetings with Remarkable Men*, the first remarkable man was his father. It's about the level of being of my teacher or my father.

I think the phrase you are referring to is that the true 'maker' is the teacher. That comes out in the chapter on Heptaparaparshinokh. My understanding in that reference he says that His Endlessness is only the maker of a 3-brained being. You get the physical person by the forces of nature, but your being is dependent on your teacher. And I think, in that context, he is pleading and hoping that any human being that is going to have an influence on you as you grow up, including your father and other people whom you would actually call a teacher, including people in Work whom you would look up to. So we can take a whole range of people who have an influence on your being in your life.

I think he specifically states that the biological father is not necessarily the maker. The teacher makes the child who he is.

(The section from Heptaparaparshinokh, page 818, and page 57 in *Meetings* are read out.)

There is also a reference in the chapter on form and sequence, page 1165. (This was read out.)

I would like to add this in the way of a cautionary note. I am reminded of a statement in, *In Search of the Miraculous*. I'll paraphrase it. It says something to the effect that "a man's not worth a brass farthing but will have no less than Jesus Christ for a teacher" and he goes on. "Man needs a teacher who has a little higher understanding than the people, but not so much higher that he cannot be understood."

Perhaps someone can provide an answer for me. We always educate our intellect and forget the other parts of ourselves, particularly the emotional centre. Ouspensky talks about balancing our centres.

Oskiano is always 3-brained in every single instance. It is never isolated to one-brained. It always must have something balanced. It is a whole experience.

Let's move on from the 1st Series to the 2nd Series

Is there a differentiation between a preparation for a responsible life and the responsible life itself? What does that mean? Does that mean to be a responsible being and how do we properly prepare for it? What do we do differently after we prepare? When we look at those early chapters to the young 'G' there comes a point where he becomes a responsible being. But it seems like there is still a great deal of accumulated wisdom and experience that follows on that and is that really Oskiano? Or is that the result of living a responsible life?

Do you think then it comes in the 3rd chapter when he begins to witness various phenomena and he asks questions from his friends and he is very dissatisfied with the answers he receives. And he concludes that ordinary education does not answer those questions. Then he begins his search for those answers.

When he begins his search, that is the responsible life.

There is the initial triad in *Meetings* with his father, Bogachevsky and Dean Borsch, and they each have certain qualities. He carries that notion of abstract questions and its that which he is seeking an answer to.

It's the highest part of the third brain that can abstract, and then build on abstractions like language, numbers, concepts, virtue, courage, faith, hope, justice and so forth. That requires the highest part. When you study the maturation of nerve pathways in the brain, it is at the age of approximately 20 to 22 in man when the pathways into what is called the prefrontal cortex have been established and finally become what is called myelinated. Myelination is a kind of insulation but it also establishes these pathways as being permanently accessible. This is a useful way to see maturation. At that point, forever in the life of that individual, there will be rapid access to these parts of the brain that make it possible for us to abstract in this highly complex way.

For me I was struck by the fact that each figure has certain characteristics, has certain interests and certain questions. Some of those characters are killed and some are still alive. He gives each one an origin, an interest; he tells the future of each one and certain of them don't make it to the end of the story. I noticed when we were discussing the Captain of the spaceship and we were asking the question, "Who is the Captain?" in the first seminar. The figure of Pogossian is called "Captain Pogossian" or Mr. X, and he is one of those figures who survive. He is still alive and runs his ships and spends all his time in the engine room with the mechanical aspects on how to run the ship.

This is an allegory on learning how to run our machine.

As far as the education goes, I am always impressed by the incredible flexibility that he had in all three centres, physical, emotional and intellectual.

The inferences are in the way he was raised by his father and his first tutor. The reason they kept changing the tasks that they gave him was so that he ended up with an interest in everything.

He could put his hand to anything with an interest, with knowing how it worked and seeing the essence of it.

G's grandmother too. She really gives him permission to be himself. She enables him in a very different way from what you learn from others.

[There follows a quotation from A&E regarding duality and reawakening - through re-education of conscience...]

If conscience was educated back into the sub-conscious, what are we about? How do we see out this question of work as a process? I am just interested to see if anybody resonates to this question.

I think you must be conscious of your sub-conscious. This is a part of the main psychological therapies, to bring the sub-conscious back.

You see, this always interests me in groups when you try to open a question and somebody immediately answers it, so that we kind of flop. But I'm interested in how we see. We're all here in the name of 'G's teaching. To me the interest would be to explore - having talked about education of children in the positive and negative aspects - but nevertheless coming to the conclusion that the sub-conscious, the conscience, has been enfolded and buried as a result of the inexorable pressure exerted by the waking consciousness aggregate of individual impulses. We are challenged by the need to 3/4 as it were 3/4 to go in every direction to reverse this process. How do you see it?

I can only give my contribution. For me my resonance has to do with this matter of subconsciousness - and the false consciousness. The old example that has been given in the Work has to do with this educational question - which is why I am on time when I have an appointment with my dentist but when I make an appointment with myself I don't keep it because nobody sees it. But that is horrifying - because it's the truth. There are so many facets. I am not even pretending to understand. Coming back, for instance, to the movements. The movements are from 'G'. They are very important. During the last class we had in The Netherlands a man - a very honest man by the way - became very emotional and we asked why. He than said I've now confronted something - a demand on my inner self that I have given up a very long time ago. We were all very moved because it's the same for us all. He said, because it was in me it was so difficult that I gave up. That is the sub-conscious that 'G' talks about. For me the inner life that nobody see - but when people see, Oh yes! That's what he calls lying. He is very direct. So behaving so that nobody sees what I really am is lying. So why do I keep appointments with other people and I have great difficulty in keeping appoints with myself?

For me this is the value of a group. Because if I don't have the will to keep that appointment, a group, by tasks, substitutes a kind of will that I don't have.

What I'm really questioning is what the kind of influence could be upon each other - which help to redress the balance.

Part of the way I see it is when I first read *In Search* for instance. I read that man cannot DO - everything happens. There was something in me that immediately accepted that as the truth and it made such sense. But my belief is in the background and it becomes the cause of much suffering when I try to make endless appointments with myself and never keep them. It's as if there is a part of me that believes that it could - and it did not - and therefore it always brings me to a place of suffering over that, and somehow my sense is that it's some sub-conscious belief- I would never have thought about it had that statement not been made. It's as if it has two aspects - my faith, my hope, or my love, or some part of my sub-conscious came to this conclusion by itself because it wasn't educated otherwise and somehow the influence of Work and Work ideas helps to penetrate that sub-conscious in a way that shows us what is not there.

With your reading from A&E, what he meant for me was the question, "How can we learn to be sincere?" And when I read that passage over and over again, I know it's true that sincerity is not part of me and how can I learn to be sincere?

Sincerity is part of your conscience.

So do you think then, if sincerity is part of my conscience, what can awaken my conscience? What do we think it is? Because for me that was almost the first step. What is the catalyst that awakens it?

I've been working on a question I've been asking myself when I think I've made a decision, "Am I being honest?" Because sometimes I realize that I'm afraid of -my own inner truth. Then I ask myself why I am afraid of that inner truth? And the reason is that it's easy to stay where I am because I am used to it and it works for me, it's convenient, and if I'm honest I have say "You need to grow up here; you need to make some shifts here; you need to dump some of this stuff this garbage that you carry around." That means I must change. That for me is the scary part but it is also my work.

'G' does actually describe this process and it starts with self observation. As you observe yourself you start to see all the things that are not right. Now arises the energy to change it and that energy leads you to be able to see even more. Then you finally become totally convinced not just on the surface with your whole being of how unbecoming you are and from that comes the true energy. So if we observe ourselves first we get an attack of conscience and the energy of conscience gives us the tool to see the real problems.

'G' said that you can observe yourself. You don't know how but you have to try. That is the start.

Before the interval we talked about how to be sincere. I said that I respect children and I said aloud - all of you heard - I was ashamed because I hear my voice and I said "I'm lying", I try to respect and I want to respect. But it's not true when I hear my voice. If I'm thinking along I'm convinced that I'm very good. And I thank you for making me see the light.
I have to approach the one thing that has been said - seriously - that's what you call garbage in yourself. That's a negative qualification.

That's what I need to let go of.

If I see something I don't like or need I cannot change.

That for me is all words. You have to make something in yourself.

I already knew that I wanted to respect everyone and I wanted to convince myself.

So it's good because I can make a goal for myself and work with it.

Let me tell you quite frankly. I have been a long time in Work. It's my honest opinion that nine out of ten people who try to be on the road that 'G' indicated make a severe mistake. Gradually what they wish to change in themselves shifts from the original impulse to what Freud would call a 'Super Ego'. They want themselves to be successful in the Work. That's a deadly trap because they forgot that you can only observe what you love.

That's exactly what I was going to say. The garbage must be loved then allowed to die. That's hard.

Then you try to change yourself.

Oh no! We don't want that.

It is seeing what it is and changing your inner life because you saw.

Now we are back to Oskiano.

Would you say then that what this lady was talking about was that there was no impartiality there? Because I want to change myself and that's impossible in the Gurdjieffian sense. Ordinarily if I want to give up smoking, I give up smoking. If I want to stop drinking coffee, I stop. All these things are ordinary. But if I want change in the 'G' sense then I must accept myself; completely.

But if you want to change yourself in the 'G' sense, that's because you wish to be aware of the forces. Smoking or no smoking - it's the vision of the forces at play.

One of the traps for me is how we use the word 'Self'. There's nothing to change - in the bigger sense - because we are this self. The mis-education causes us to take the self as everything that is now, all of this personality. That's why we don't want to free the self.

I would like to read - since the expression of the relationship between waking consciousness and the sub-consciousness seems to be very much associated with the question. This is from the chapter on hypnotism. [Begins to read] I would submit that one way of understanding the hypnotic state not brought about by the use of hanbledzoin but by this special means of hindering the blood vessels is exactly the plethora of work methods created by 'G'.

Say that again.

I would submit that this which hinders the difference in filling the blood vessels and opens the door to bringing the sub-conscious into functioning simultaneously with the waking consciousness - exactly the aim that we have - is brought about by, as he mentions, this special means and this special means I would submit, perhaps, is all the work methods that 'G' has left for us. The denial exercise, the giving-up, self-observation, the struggle with negativity. In every single case a friction is produced if one makes the effort. And that friction is precisely between waking consciousness and sub-consciousness. To try and bring them into a state where they are here and we see in both directions at once rather than not seeing the motivation and so forth. This would be the real education as we bring in this warped imbalanced circumstance and we can begin to see that our reality has this waking and sub-conscious that must be together.

On the fourth trip to the Earth and this man Belcultassi, there's a paragraph here where he is trying, trying to look at himself sincerely. And as far as he can do it, he gets to the point where he can put himself into the position of others. That's the best we can do.

End of Session

Where Do We Go From Here?

Facilitator: Sy Ginsburg

Introduction: Sy Ginsburg, Facilitator:

(Note from the Facilitator: As facilitator, I have been given the responsibility of transcribing this final conference session of *All and Everything* 2001. As in the previous year, the session was recorded so that there could be a record of the comments of the participants for the purpose of future planning. Also, as in the previous year, requests were made that the transcript of this session be severely edited and that the comments not be identified with the participants who made them in order to allow the maximum freedom of expression. Consequently, neither the names of the commentators nor the names of any specific persons to whom a commentator referred appear here.

There were some difficulties in transcribing this session. Because of the placement of the microphones, because of mechanical hiss in the recording equipment, and because people were speaking from all over the room, numerous comments were not sufficiently clear on the tape to be transcribed. In some instances the words could not be understood at all I believe this had to do with proximity to a microphone and also because some people spoke in a very soft voice. My apologies to those whose comments are not included for these reasons. In other instances only part of the comment could be understood but the gist of the comment was clear. In those cases I have summarized the comment often putting different words to it than what was probably actually said, and in this respect have taken great liberties with the transcription. I have nevertheless attempted to reproduce the substance of the session as closely as possible. There are undoubtedly errors of omission, misinterpretation, and incorrect summarization of the comments made. I accept the responsibility for these and ask pardon.

As requested, I have not identified participants with their comments and have simply labelled each comment as attributed to a "Participant." I have attempted to include all the critical comments that were audible so that these can be considered in the planning of future conferences, but have only included specific positive comments where they might bear on the arrangement of future conferences. For the purpose of conciseness I have for the most part not included comments which appeared to be repetitious of something previously said, and I have not included the many general comments made by participants who thanked the planners and others for their efforts. In the instances of my own comments, when they have been of a substantive nature. I have identified myself as a participant as are all the others who offered comments. In the instances of my making a procedural statement, I have indicated myself as the Facilitator. It is my hope that participants and other readers will agree, the importance of the comments lies in their content and not in the attribution to whoever made them).

Facilitator: This morning is an open forum. The topic is "Where Do We Go From Here." What we have done in past years is to simply go around the room for your comments and impressions about the conference. Please do not be afraid to say anything negative because many of those kinds of comments are useful in planning another conference. Even though the session is being recorded so that the Planning Committee will have a record of the comments, names will not be attributed to what is said. Please feel free to speak. After we have gone around the room and everyone has given their impressions, then we will try to come to some sort of tentative conclusions and directions for another conference.

As you all know, this conference is not a work group, it is not an organization, and it is not an umbrella group. It is simply a group of people getting together in pursuit of our mutual interest in *All and Everything*, however we understand that. Whatever conclusions and directions we come to, the Planning Committee will try to implement as best as it can based upon these comments and the experiences from the previous conferences.

Participant: I think that people who make presentations should have a good loud voice, have good pronunciation, and should present good information. I also think, as another person suggested to me, that we should consider studying all three series of *All and Everything* at the same time. On my computer, I can search a word in *All and Everything* and find out about it in different places. We should also ask people to prepare better in advance for the discussions in the seminars.

Facilitator: I would like to interject that anyone who wants to comment on what was said by this participant or upon any other remarks to be made by other participants should please feel free to do so.

Participant: I think that having the music is critical to the conference. I also think that the seminar where the facilitator changed the usual procedure was not very successful because it took away from discussing the content of those chapters. I think facilitators and presenters should stick to *All and Everything*.

Participant: I agree with most everything you said. I am really not interested in hearing someone quote from some other book that they read. I would like us to stay within our context unless it is of scholarly interest as to the origins of Mr. Gurdjieff's material.

Participant: I also feel it is a waste of time to discuss material at the level of gossip. It almost reaches a level of titillation, like "who said this in 1948" and so on. We miss the point when we do that.

Participant: My personal preference in the seminars is that we approach the chapters numerically, and I do prefer the shortened time for the presentations.

All & Everything Conference 2001

Participant: I believe we should do some kind of practice at the conference because *All and Everything* is about how to work. I was very surprised that at the sittings in the morning we are only two or three persons. I propose we have some kind of movements. I also think we should have a session where we speak about our personal work. And there are not enough young people here.

Participant: I agree with all sorts of criticisms made and things that could be improved, but what could hardly be improved for me was what the conference gave to me. I really am grateful for this conference because I see how in ordinary life how weak I am. And I see that other people here have the same interests and that they are necessary for my own growth. One of the consequences of the organ Kundabuffer is that I am arrogant and think I do not need the efforts of others, but I do.

I was very grateful for one of the presentations and for the reminiscences of that presenter's experiences in the work. It was an absolute highlight of my life. Where do you see such a man! And touching his wooden constructions was so good, so real. Was such an event useful for my inner work? Yes it was!

Participant: I feel that one of the most important things at the conference was everyone who was here. The group dynamics is what makes this conference work.

Participant: This new people business is important. But I object when this conference is used by people to draw recruits for their particular activities. This is something for the Planning Committee to be concerned with.

Participant: The conference is overloaded with intellectual material. There should be more emphasis on other aspects.

Participant: I am grateful to be here. I needed to be here. A highlight was the honesty. When people came from their heart that was the most important part of the conference. The hardest part of the conference is when people got wrapped up in their heads and lost their heart. I would like to see more of the demonstration of the movements because I have not had the opportunity of learning about and doing the movements. I understand the difficulty of someone attempting to do a movement alone when it is really a group movement. Being from an art school background that is how I learn so the visual experience was important. Also the slide presentation of the building in Paris was visual and so a highlight for me.

Participant: A participant who could not be here for this session asked me to say that he comes here for the friendships.

Another participant who had to leave early asked me to say the following. That it is good to have people who have read many thousands of books as well as others who have not read any. Also that the session leaders should talk less, use fewer words. Proposed papers to be presented should be better prepared because otherwise it is too time consuming for those who cannot control verbosity. We should build on what we have in future conferences and we do not need to go look for famous names. If we are looking for prestige names on our stationary then we have not learned from Mr. Gurdjieff. If we should be so fortunate as to have a surplus of good papers proposed in a future conference there would be nothing wrong with having two groups going on at the same time as they do at academic conferences.

For myself I think it has been a wonderful experiment to meet without rules, but I think we need a few rules in order to better respect each other's point of view. For example, if you want to partake and speak in a seminar such as on Oskiano, you must read the material or otherwise just listen.

Mr. Gurdjieff talked to all three centers. He taught from three centers. We should consider this in future conferences.

Participant: I said at the beginning of the conference that I had no expectations, but I found that I had some. I expected that people would be bringing parts of their individual work to share. I enjoyed the demonstration of movements. That was special for me and also the first paper on higher-being-bodies. I was bemused by the way the book was studied in the seminars. It could be approached better.

A question that came up in one of the seminars was: What is being-Partkdolg-duty? I received the impression that we are struggling to work but we do not quite know what work is. Maybe this is a question for the conference to look at: Do we know what work is and what we are trying to achieve?

Participant: I would like in the conference to compare the old *Beelzebub's Tales* with the new *Beelzebub's Tales*.

I have participated in an internet chat room and I think it is an excellent tool.

Participant: I think that is a good idea because it is a way to reach out to people who are unaware of the conference.

Participant: I can see the general usefulness of the internet, but my experience during the past year has given me confirmation of the previous attitude Iliad that the use of email has no atmosphere. And it allows for too much to come into communications that would not be said if people were sitting in the same room. Email is a useful way to transfer data to people so that they can ponder on it. But for myself I do not see participating in a back and forth exchange.

Participant: Some things will stay with me. Because we had the demonstration of the movements, it communicated with us in another way. There is warmth that is probably not expressible. I think that the discussions together and being together went very deeply for all of us. Another thing that will always stay with me and that I can share with other people, is the hope that one Presenter conveyed from his experiences with Mr. Gurdjieff that conveyed faith, belief and optimism. It is the antidote to Ouspensky's pessimism. I am one of the people who does not have a group so I carry these things a long way. That presenter also brought his sculptures for everyone to look at and pass around and this was very educational for me and for others.

Being part of the Planning Committee I know that it is very difficult to organize this conference. The Planning Committee does try to take into consideration the needs of everyone as much as we can, and the Planning Committee does care about everyone who comes here.

This conference is called *All and Everything*. People have criticized the head brain but this written material is Gurdjieff's legacy to us so it requires us to give it the best possible treatment that it deserves and this does require an intellectual effort. We cannot just go by feelings.

Participant: I would like first to address the question of new people. In the review of the Russian *Beelzebub's Tales*, Gurdjieff himself says he would like to be addressed only as Monsieur or Mister. And the sole title he gave himself is "teacher of dances." His teaching was not widely known in his lifetime as he avoided all notoriety. I think that is very important because I don't think proselytizing is the way. We have referred to people who come back year after year. But this is no guaranty that new people will come. They simply need to be attracted by what is going on here.

I agree with everything that has been said. The only thing I would like to add is that the one seminar that has been criticized because it was handled so differently, was useful because it caused us all to participate with each other in small groups. I think that kind of format could be useful in a future conference. It enabled people who do not normally speak in a large group to be able to participate and find their level.

On the subject of using the mind, the use of my mind has not been my training. As a child I was not trained to use my mind. But over the last two years I have realized that if I don't use it then I cannot be a three-brained being, and cannot receive the input that helps me to become balanced. So, anything that would help those of us, who are not scientists and who are not mathematicians, to learn more, would be helpful.

Also, I think a more organized meditation a couple of times a day would be useful and would keep the energy high.

Participant: I was at the conference last year as well as this. What I enjoyed the most about the conference last year was the way I felt that the thinking about the boundaries of Gurdjieff's work was expanded, as for example in the talk about astrology and *All and Everything*. This year it was the music that really gave me a lot of pleasure. And also to be able to learn about the effect of the dancing on the physical which I always wondered about. Apart from that I think the idea of a theme rather than chronological chapters is the best way to work on the contents.

Where Do We Go From Here?

(At this point in the discussion, a coffee break was taken).

Participant: The conference gives us the opportunity to share some impressions about how we react. There is the story about the man who made everyone crazy in the group. He went away and Gurdjieff went out and paid him and got him to come back. There is the story Mrs. Popoff tells about a woman. She was a newspaper editor, a big, big Russian woman. When she would come into the meetings she would interrupt everything with whatever she was upset about. Mrs. Popoff said she would keep her here under all circumstances. She really made us work on our self.

I think that limiting the talks to twenty minutes with more time for questions and answers is a good addition. It was mentioned earlier by someone that people should be more prepared. I think that is good. It is something I see in my self that I need to be more prepared. I needed to be more prepared to talk about *Meetings with Remarkable Men* that came up in the discussions.

Participant: With regard to doing the chapters of *Beelzebub's Tales* in sequence, every synagogue in the world reads the Five Books of Moses in sequence from the beginning to the end in one year. So, going by chapter is not an unusual way.

Participant: I just wanted to say something about the theme of "Oskiano". When we talked about taking that theme I only realized later how immense that theme was.

Participant: At least for newer people, going by chapters is helpful because they can read the designated chapters. But to come up with a theme like "Oskiano", if you don't have a lot of knowledge already, even *The Guide and Index* won't help much because it is too big. So, maybe seminars on both, a theme and chapters is the way to go.

Participant: As regards a theme versus the chapters, there are so many secrets in the form in a single chapter, that just one chapter by itself contains so much; it would be a shame to lose that. On the other hand by taking a theme we can integrate more parts of the *Tales*. So, it is worthwhile to think in terms of both.

One observation I have is that I have always gone away from the conference feeling very positive because there were so many new directions opened up for me. We should not have a sense of incompletion. I always leave with all the questions that I was never smart enough to ask, but that somebody else asked and that starts me in a new direction. I have a gold mine that I am going home with. New impressions and new ways to look at different things: the text, movements, there are so many different things. I think this is such an important aspect of the conference for all of us.

Participant: It seems to me that most of the time of the conference is spent with us using words to comment on, to criticize, to analyze. But it is supplemented by other things than words, like the sculptures. So, we can help one another to perceive things like the message behind the words. It is important to give thought to how you go beyond the words.

All & Everything Conference 2001

Participant: This conference has evolved into something that is all about relationship. There is a relationship between all of us when we gather together. For me that is the structure that holds it together. The richness of having people come from different countries and different cultures has been for me a wonderful, wonderful gift.

Participant: For next year I will have to bring a few more jokes. When organizing the conference there are always a lot of things to do, but when I come I realize it is such a small price to pay. The conference moves my center of gravity on every level. I have this same experience every year that it moves my psychological center of gravity. There are so many questions and so much new energy that I go away with.

Participant: One participant who could not be at this session asked me to say that while sometimes it cannot be helped, it is not a good idea in general for people to "fly in and fly out" of here just for a day. In a certain sense they are being unfair to the people who are here for the whole time. At the same time, they are not getting all the benefit they could. So, we should urge people to participate for the whole conference.

For myself, I realized about halfway through the conference just how valuable it is. There is nothing like it anywhere on this planet in so far as studying and approaching Mr. Gurdjieff's work, and I thought about how much would be lost if for some reason these conferences did not continue.

At the first conference and even at the first and second conferences we were, in a sense, all new people. What has happened by this sixth conference is that relationships have developed between people who keep attending and for those of us who are here on a repeat basis we know how valuable that is. At the same time I feel that it is important, not to go for size which I no longer think is important, but to have the continuing insights inputted by other people. I am very grateful for the insights into the Tales that I have received here from people from many countries and cultures. In our groups in the United States I continue to be surprised by insights that people come up with. But it is even more valuable here because we come from all over. This really is an international thing and collectively we can bring more to it. So, I think it is important to make whatever efforts we can to have more new people from all over. I do not think we did a very good job this year of making the effort to find more new people to participate.

I want to mention that because of the use of email during the past year, several of us were able to exchange ideas on a particular topic. In this case it was on the topic of higher-being-bodies. This led to papers being presented on this subject. It is very much different from email chat rooms where everyone just goes blah, blah, blah. So, I hope the email list that has been passed around will stimulate those who wish to converse on some particular subject of interest.

Facilitator: Now that everyone has had a chance to comment on the conference, the next part of this discussion will be to try to make some specific tentative ideas about where do we go from here?

Where Do We Go From Here?

The first general question that we ask every year is: Do we want another conference? Please let us have a show of hands.

(All hands were raised).

Does anyone not want another conference next year?

(No hands were raised).

Does anyone want to skip next year and have another conference the year after?

(No hands were raised).

Does anyone want to consider changing the time of the year?

Participant: This is a good time of the year because the travel rates are still low. I would like to have it even earlier but I am a committee of one.

Facilitator: A point of information is that next year Easter falls on Sunday, March 31, 2002. In general costs go up close to and after Easter for air fares and hotel rates, and it is spring vacation time from schools. Historically, we have had the conferences quite early. The first year (1996) the conference was held in February. If we want to time the conference the same next year as this year then we would have to have the conference two weeks before Easter again. This means two weeks earlier than now.

Participant: For me this is the best time of the year because it is not so cold.

Facilitator: Would anybody want to have the conference at a completely different time of the year such as August or September?

(There were no responses to this).

Facilitator: This brings us to the next question that was asked earlier. Would you ask that question again?

Participant: Would we want to have the conference here or in the United States?

Participant: The United States cannot begin to compete with the prices here. The air fares seem to be cheaper from the United States to Europe. Also the room prices are much less here unless you go 100 or 200 miles away from a big city in the states.

Participant: I think the idea would be that if we were to have the conference in the United States again, we would look for some type of retreat that holds seminars.

Participant: Since last year I have changed my mind. Some of it has to do with the economics, but some of it is that we have really planted a seed here.

Participant: I think that the amount of foreigners, that is the amount of non-U. S. people who came to the conference in the United States in Portland last year were not acceptable. If we have it there again it will become a U. S. conference, not an international conference.

Participant: A lot of the people who came to Portland were from our group and they could not afford to come here. So, we didn't get hoards of people from all over the United States last year, but we did also have some people from Salt Lake and from Texas.

Participant: But some of those people have now come here, so we did gain some people for here.

Participant: I don't think it is geography so much as it is desire.

Participant: It strikes me that the conference in the United States was a sort of North American conference. We call this an international conference and I think that England in particular, I am not talking about France or other European places or Australia or other places outside the U. S., but England with access to these big London airports really makes it international. This is probably because Europe is a relatively small place so people from elsewhere in Europe will come here and at the same time we see that people from North America are willing to come here. You told me that your airfare to come here (directing this comment to a particular person) is no more than your airfare to California.

Participant: Here, I feel good coming.

Participant: How many came to the U. S. from Europe last year? Only four.

Participant: We are fortunate that we found this place, the Royal Norfolk, six years ago.

Participant: The only problem would be if it goes into receivership or the next owner raises the prices. It has had quite a few owners already.

Facilitator: Maybe we should take a vote on this if everyone is done. All in favour of having it here again next year at the Royal Norfolk raise your hands.

(All hands appeared to be raised).

Participant: As someone here said, this place is shabby chic.

Facilitator: There is another question. Does anyone feel that the conference should be either longer or shorter than beginning on Wednesday evening and ending at Sunday noon? The first year, 1996 if some of you will remember, it was one day shorter.

Where Do We Go From Here?

Participant: Would it be an advantage to begin the conference Wednesday morning and end it Sunday morning?

Participant: I think that for the people who are regularly employed, we would be cutting even more into their work week.

Participant: For people coming here from across the pond, even if their planes get in at 7:00 a.m., they are tired when they get here. Even if they could get here for a conference starting at noon, I am assuming they don't want to pay for an extra day, they are tired, and they need a nap.

(The discussion on this subject waned and no vote was taken on changing the length of the conference).

Facilitator: These are nuts and bolts questions that we have been talking about, and the Planning Committee will deal with these as best they can. If anyone has any other of these kinds of matters to bring up please do so. I have one matter and that is that we recognize that we did not do a good job this year of attracting new people. If anyone has any expertise in how to do this, their help would be appreciated.

Participant: Just sending pieces of paper to a general list is not good. People get so much of this kind of mail. I just stand by the recycle bin when I go through my mail and toss most of it away immediately. You could better use the internet. Also, it was suggested to send letters to heads of groups asking them to speak to their group members, but not to hand their group members a coupon because these leaders do not want to lose control of their groups. Also, a lot of groups are just not interested. They feel they don't need this.

Participant: We need to make a list of group leaders to whom a letter could be sent. The letter should be drafted in a way that it will not be tossed out and there might be some people in various groups who have a special interest in *All and Everything*.

Participant: The letter should be sort of a "we need you" letter.

Participant: We need to accumulate a list of names and addresses of group leaders, and they are all over the world. Some people lead groups of five people and some lead groups of fifty people.

Participant: There is also the idea of getting some publicity in these magazines. *Stopinder* was mentioned. *Telos* was mentioned. I am not talking about a paid ad which is expensive but rather an announcement. We only tried a paid ad once, in *Gnosis*, which has since gone out of business. It cost $400 and did not bring one response.

Participant: We are talking about writing an article for these magazines or a letter to the editor.

All & Everything Conference 2001

Participant: The groups I know, if they receive a letter they will reject it. So, I think it is better to contact people personally. I still know them. I have already talked to some people informally. I can direct them to go to the website of the conference.

Participant: What about a task for every person who has attended here to speak personally to one other person who they feel would be interested in attending?

Participant: Surely, no one will object to that and we have talked about it for two years in a row. But in the main, I think that we will grow in exactly the same way as work groups grow, through personal contact. Most of us came into contact with a group through a personal contact, not through a newspaper ad.

Participant: What about the people who have come here before but no longer do. I remember one man from Washington, D.C.

Participant: The Planning Committee has a list of people who have previously attended. It is a little over one hundred.

Participant: People who remember those people should personally contact them.

Participant: Since I have been responsible for doing the mailings, if any of you make a personal contact and then want a follow up, if you will email me such names I will put them on the mailing list to get the newsletter and the invitation. This is an open conference so it is open to anyone within reason. We have sent out a newsletter each year in the summer to the entire mailing list. It is now about 350 names of which only about 100 have attended the previous conferences, and we never hear from the other 250. It has been suggested that when we send out a newsletter this spring or summer that we put a coupon in there saying that if you want to continue to receive this newsletter and invitation, to please return the coupon. Otherwise the name will be removed from the mailing list.

Participant: I came because you sent me that application form and the hotel brochure. It was in my face and all I had to do was to do it. The hotel brochure was important. I needed it to make the reservations.

Participant: One of the problems for this year was that we did not get enough of the hotel brochures from the hotel so we could not send a brochure to everyone to whom an invitation was sent.

Participant: Somehow we have to encourage people to submit papers early. How do we do that? Maybe we should put something into the Proceedings regarding the next conference giving the dates and site at Bognor for next year and saying that it is very important to submit papers early.

Participant: Also, we can try to get the Newsletter out sooner than we have in the past.

Where Do We Go From Here?

Participant: We should make the closing date for submissions earlier. It should be in December. That gives us January to make a selection.

Participant: It is always going to be a last minute thing. How many reservations did we have just a short time ago, three or four!

Participant: People made hotel reservations but we only got three or four registration coupons sent in before the conference began.

Participant: Another thing, if anyone here has any website expertise we could use some help on this, like establishing links to other websites.

Participant: Has everyone who wants to be on it, signed up on the email list for exchanging emails during the year. There are fifteen names on it as of now.

Participant: May I suggest that the Planning Committee simply send one email to whoever is on the list simply giving the listing of email addresses. Then it will be up to those people to contact each other as they wish to discuss a subject or whatever.

Participant: Why not also send three suggested themes. Then it will be up to those who are interested to sign up to discuss one of these themes.

Participant: I would like to suggest that we in the U.S. look around in our areas for a place to have the next conference in 2003.

Facilitator: Every year is a new year.

Facilitator: If there are no other final comments, may I suggest that we quiet ourselves for a few minutes to end this conference, All and Everything 2001.

End of Session

Appendix 1 - Review of Beelzebub's Tales to His Grandson in Russian

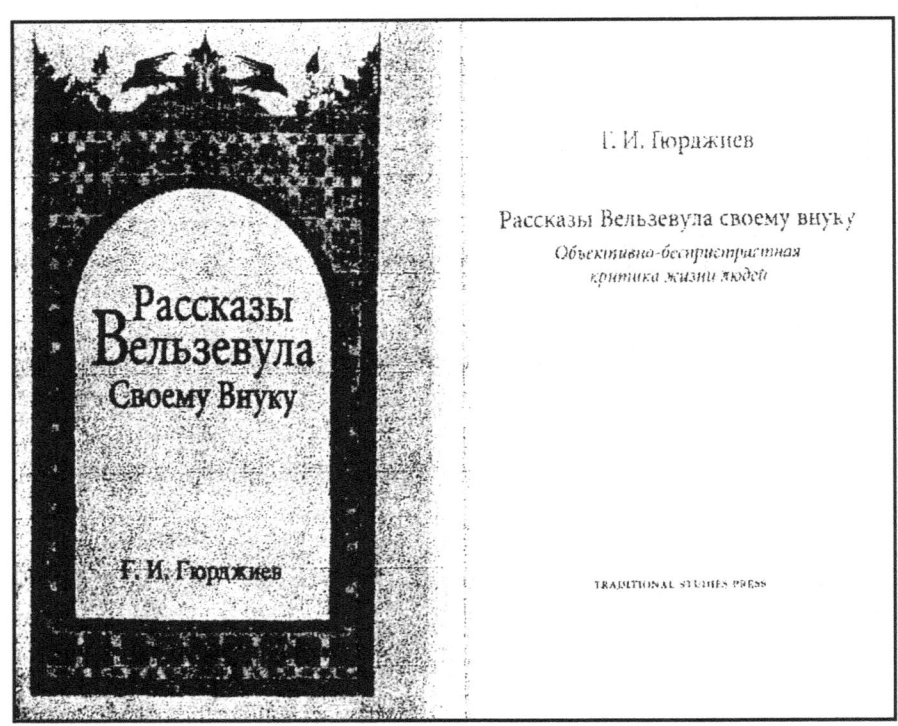

Front of the dust jacket and the title page of the volume

РАССКАЗЫ ВЕЛЬЗЕВУЛА СВОЕМУ ВНУКУ
Объективно-беспристрастная критика жизни людей by Г. И. ГЮРДЖИЕВ.

First Series of **ВСЁ И ВСЯ** (= ALL AND EVERYTHING). Hardcover, size: 18.5 x 12.25 x 4.5 cm, Volume of 1227 + 18 pages, with a Preface (in Russian) by Dr. Michel de Salzmann.

First Edition, Copyright @ Triangle Editions, Inc., 2000. Published by the TRADITIONAL STUDIES PRESS, Toronto, Canada, ISBN: 0919608116. When released, the retail sale price will be $47.

Appendix 1 - Review of Beelzebub's Tales to His Grandson in Russian

УРА! УРА! УРА! = HURRAH! HURRAH! HURRAH!

At long last the hitherto jealously guarded original Russian text *of Beelzebub's Tales to His Grandson* has been released and published, so that now it is available to anyone who can read Russian.

This First Russian edition has been prepared by a small international group assembled by Dr. Michel de Salzmann, using all the known surviving typescripts, including those found in the personal papers of the late Olga de Hartmann (1885 - 1979), some of which were even still in the "old" Russian spelling.

As Dr. Michel de Salzmann, who signs it as the President of the Gurdjieff Foundation in Paris, writes (in Russian) in his preface to this first edition in the original Russian of *Beelzebub's Tales to His Grandson*: "Notwithstanding that this book has been already published in 12 languages and is known in the whole world, in Russian - its original language - it appears only now, 50 years after its author's death and 66 years after it was written.[1] It is impossible not to be surprised by this. Undoubtedly, for a long time external conditions and demands of the moment screened such a paradoxical situation, but, instead of looking for the reasons for this, let us rejoice that at long last Gurdjieff's teachings appear in the author's own tongue."

Let us note that, wisely, as Dr. Michel de Salzmann points out in his Preface, it was decided to continue using in this edition in Russian the now obsolete letter **Ѳ** in the spelling of some special words, in particular in **Ѳеомортмалогос** = Theomertmalogos. In modem Russian this letter **Ѳ** has the sound of **FF**.

But, regrettably, in certain other words the unfortunate final editorial decision was to accept the communist soviet's meddling with Russian grammar, whereby, amongst other changes, they replaced the etymologically necessary and correct prefix **без = bez**, meaning "without", **by бес = bes**, which happens to be one of the three Russian words for "devil"! The most frequent designation given by Beelzebub to the Supreme Being is ENDLESSNESS, in Russian **БЕЗКОНЧНЫЙ**, meaning "without end" when spelt "correctly", but when spelt as **БЕСКОНЧНЫЙ**, by assonance suggests the meaning: "undoubted devil"!

Also, although as a general rule every Russian letter has but one sound, there are some exceptions, one of them being that the letter written **e** and normally pronounced as the **ye** in **ye**s, in some words is pronounced as the **yo** in **yo**lk. In such cases it was customary, in the "old" spelling, to indicate this variation in pronunciation by placing the two diaeretic dots above the letter, thus: **ё**. The now used "new" soviet spelling, though, has dispensed with this; in all but one case it does

---

[1] A footnote appended here states: "Several translations from the English edition began to appear in Russia in the 80s. They were incomplete, bore no resemblance to the original language and were printed without the permission of "The Triangle Editions" who hold the rights to the publication of all Gurdjieff's writings."

not matter much as the word's correct pronunciation would have been learnt by usage, but in one particular case it does matter: the word which in Russian means "all" or "everything" before certain words is pronounced normally, as for instance in **все книги** meaning "all the books", but in **все дальнейнјее** meaning "everything further" the **е** must be pronounced as the **уо** in y**о**lk. It is not a problem to fluent speakers of Russian, who know through practice when to pronounce the **e** in **все** as **ye** and when to pronounce it as **yo**, but for those who have learned Russian only recently this would not be always immediately evident; thus they would in many cases use the wrong pronunciation, that is, the wrong sound-vibration, which is most important in order to speak Russian correctly and perhaps also on another level. The right pronunciation/vibration is important also for the 'second' reading, which should be aloud (the Russian text clearly says: "as if for someone listening"). What is particularly surprising in this decision, is that the Russian for 'ALL AND EVERYTHING" is **ВСЁ И ВСЯ**, the first word, having no context as a guide, to be pronounced correctly *must*, to make sense in Russian, be spelt **ВСЁ** (with the diaeresis ¨ above the **Ё**).

Apart from these few imperfections, it is great to have at last the possibility to know exactly what Mister Gurdjieff really wrote and exactly how he spelt his *hapax legomena*.[2] Now that we have Mr. G's own written words in the original, perhaps we can, and should, quite legitimately speculate on what the original of this unusual book can bring to the careful and attentive reader. Thus, *The Arousing of Thought* seems to me to be one of its purposes, right from the start. So, here goes:

___

[2] For a definition of this term, see *The Great Oxford Dictionary, The Random House Dictionary Of The English Language* or any other good dictionary.

Appendix 1 - Review of Beelzebub's Tales to His Grandson in Russian

Is it significant that the Russian title has four words, the third one (CBOEMY) being really wholly redundant, the meaning of the title remaining precisely the same without it? Did Mr. G decide to use 4 and not 3 words because numerologically 4 is the number of stability and authority? Note that the fourth Tarot Major Arcanum is called THE EMPEROR ("Magical Title" is "Sun of the Morning: Chief Among the Mighty").

The sub-title has five words. Is that because 5 is traditionally "the number of man" and arithmosophically signifies life, struggle and change? The fifth Tarot Major Arcanum is called THE HIEROPHANT ("The Magus of the Eternal Gods"), that is, "the Revealer of Mysteries".

Together the title and sub-title add to nine words; the number 9 refers to aim, understanding, conclusion and reward. It is also the number of the Enneagram. In the Tarot the ninth Major Arcanum is called THE HERMIT ("The Prophet of the Eternal: Magus of the Voice of the Power of Light") and represents the man who has reached the summit of achievement and spiritual perfection possible to Man and lights the way for those who follow him.[3]

Astrologically, in a Horoscope, the 9th House, though Cadent, is described as individual and internal, being the ultimate extension of the 1st House (relating to the planetary body), of the 4th House (concerning the end of human life) and of the 5th House (governing the psychic nature and its Kesdjan body) and thus the 9th House represents the "Highest-Being-Body", that is, man's Soul and his potential, temporally and spiritually. It presides over the exploration of space, time and the realms of metaphysics, being the House of Philosophy, the higher and abstract mind, and the Objective Reason, hence of all that concerns the scientific and religious attitudes. In addition, together with the 4th House, it represents the future more than the past (which is included in the

---

[3] For a more advanced numerological analysis, see Nicolas Tereshchenko's *Suggested Numerological Structure of Beelzebub's Tales* (which is a chapter of his, unpublished in English, *Mister Gurdjieff and the Fourth Way*) in *ALL AND EVERYTHING 1996 PROCEEDINGS*, p. 185.

5th House) or the present (which is part of the 1st House) and rules dreams, imagination, prophecy, thought and visions, as well as intuition and the intellect.[4]

Thus, apparently, the title page itself subtly informs our "subconscious" that the *Tales* contain all the essential knowledge needed to allow all men to reach the optimum state of Being possible to them, this transmission being made under the highest Secular and Spiritual Authorities acting together in harmonic synarchy and synergic syzygy.

As well as on a numerological and an astrological bases, the *Tales* seem to be constructed as a set of interlocking enneagrams[5] and certainly also contain other carefully veiled and as yet undetected symbols.

Many very different opinions are held about Mister Gurdjieff. Some have seen him as nothing but an impostor, a pretender to occult knowledge, a charlatan or even a "black magician"; some called him a "Mystic", a "Genius", or a genuine and inspired "Teacher"; others believed in him as a reliable and wise "Mentor" who knows all the answers[6] and as the "Guide on the Way of Return"; and a few recognized him as a High "Initiate" and a real "Master", even, perhaps, a genuine "Messenger" sent from "Above". But he himself insisted to be addressed only as "Monsieur" or "Mister" (Focnonm = Gospodin in Russian) and the sole title he ever claimed for himself is "Teacher of Dances".[7] His Teaching was not widely known in his lifetime, as he avoided all notoriety or proselytism. But he managed nevertheless to transmit an entirely practical way of Work-on-Self, solidly based on a coherent theoretical basis (which he called "Objective Science") and with techniques and exercises of proven efficiency. This practical method Mr. G called "**Haïda** Yoga"[8] and "The Way of the Sly Man", as well as "The Fourth Way", but now it is commonly referred to as simply "The Work". He had a sure and deep knowledge of the Laws of Creation, of Conservation and of Maintenance of the Universe, a unique synthesis of Occidental and Oriental Traditions coming directly from "pre-sands Egypt", the Primordial Source of all genuine Knowledge. Moreover, he also had a deep understanding of human psychology, which made it possible for him to always know exactly what a particular follower/pupil needed to experience right here and now in order to obtain an expansion of Consciousness and perhaps even to "wake-up", were it but for a brief moment.

---

[4] See also Dr. Sophia Wellbeloved's doctoral thesis on *Gurdjieff, Astrology and Beelzebub's Tales* and her *Numbers, the Zodiac and the Tales* in ALL AND EVERYTHING 2000 PROCEEDINGS, page 49.
[5] Cf. *The Enneagrammatic Structure of Beelzebub's Tales* by Dr. Keith Buzzell in ALL AND EVERYTHING 1996 PROCEEDINGS, page 40.
[6] Cf. Ouspensky's *In Search of the Miraculous*, p. 12: "...the assurance of a specialist..."
[7] Yes, of **dances** not of "dancing"
[8] **Haïda** is an Ukranian word meaning: "Be quick! Get on with it! At the double!"

Appendix 1 - Review of Beelzebub's Tales to His Grandson in Russian

As all those who have read attentively the definitive edition of de Hartmann's autobiography[9] already know, in Russian Mr. G's family name is spelt **Гюрджиев** the second letter, **Ю**, being pronounced exactly like the English alphabet name of the letter **U** or as the **u** in **pure**, NOT as **oo** in **poor**. And the last three letters should be fully pronounced separately, each with its own sound: **и** as the **i** in **hit**, **е** as the **ye** in **yes**, and **в** as the **v** in **van**, NOT as an **ff** sound; nor must the **не** = **ie** be run together into one sound.

George Gurdjieff, the first-born of several children, was born at the midnight hour beginning the Friday 1st of January (in the Julian calendar then used in Russia, which, in the Gregorian calendar, was January 12th in the 19th century, January 13th in the 20th century and in this 21st century is January 14th), most probably in 1866[10] (though other authors/searchers propose 1864, 1872, 1877 and even 1878), in the small township of GUMRU (later renamed ALEXANDROPOL, changed in 1924 to LENINAKAN and now, since 1991, called KUMAYRI).

His father was Greek and his mother Armenian. Thus he had from childhood to learn three entirely different languages: his father's old Greek, his mother's early 19th century Armenian and the "official" Russian of a 100 years ago. The family had originally been well to do, but had suffered unforeseen reverses and so, when he was about seven years old, moved to the bigger city of KARS, where Mr. G's father began to earn his living as a carpenter and George received his basic education.

After travelling far and wide for many years in search of the answers to his many questions about why the Universe was created and in particular on the meaning of human life on Earth (as he recounts in his "Second Series": *Meetings with Remarkable Men*), in 1912 Mr. G began teaching in Moscow and St. Petersburg what he found. In 1922, after many vicissitudes due to the Russian Revolution, he finally settled in France, where, after nominating his star pupil, Madame Jeanne de Salzmann (1889 - 1990), as his successor, he died on Saturday the 29th October 1949. His body is buried in the Avon cemetery, between those of his beloved mother and wife. This grave bears no name, but there is a menhir at each end of it and also a marble bench under a tree, for those who wish to sit there quietly in silent contemplation. Mister Gurdjieff's body may be dead and buried, but his Spirit, his Teaching and the Work's Practical Method, with their special energy which he brought to our ailing world, live on, in particular in the pages of *Beelzebub's Tales to His Grandson*.

On Tuesday the 8th of July 1924 Mr. G was severely injured in a rather mysterious car accident, and, once recovered, he closed his Institute, and began to put his teachings in writing, in Russian,

---

[9] *Our Life with Mr. Gurdjieff*, definitive edition, Arkana Penguin Books, 1992. On page 140, Mr. G's name in Russian, but in its "old" spelling: **Гюрджіевъ**, appears in the illustration of the Cover design drawn by Alexander de Salzmann in Tiilis, 1919, for the prospectus of the Institute offering courses in the Science of the Harmonic Development of Man.

[10] *Gurdjieff: The Anatomy of a Myth - A Biography* by James Moore, Element Books Limited, 1991; pages 9 and 339.

in the form of a "science-fiction" story. The first chapter of the first of the three projected "series" of books suggests that some of the text would be written in Armenian. In actual fact, even if any part of the work had ever been written in that language, no part of his writings in Armenian now exists; all that we have is written in a somewhat old-fashioned Russian. In Mr. G's then Paris flat, at 47 Boulevard Pereire, the first page of "The Conversation of the Old Devil with the Young One" (as Mr. G first called what is now the "first series" of the trilogy with the overall title of "ALL AND EVERYTHING") was dictated to Olga de Hartmann on the 16th December 1924. The work's first draft was completed by November 1927, but Mr. G continued to revise parts of it right up to shortly before his death.[11]

Jeanne de Salzmann   **George Ivanovich Gurdjieff** *circa* **1931**   **Olga de Hartmann**

This "First Series", now called *Beelzebub's Tales to his Grandson* (with the most important sub-title: "*An Objectively Impartial Criticism of the Life of Men*"), was first published, in English, in 1950, that is, after Mr. G's death. The French translation (said to have been made from a later "revision" and thus rendering some of Mr. G's expressions more correctly) was issued in 1956. A second English version was published in 1992, but seems to have been "translated", at least partly, from the French rather than from the original Russian.

"All the keys are in Beelzebub" - affirmed Mr. G - "but they are not near their locks."[12]

---

[11] Personal communication to me by the late lamented Madame Jeanne de Salzmann, to explain some of the differences between the French and the first English translations.

[12] In her *The Fiery Fountains* (Horizon Press, New York, 1969) Margaret Anderson writes (p. 132): "All the keys to the enigma were perhaps offered in Gurdjieff's manuscript but, as the author said, they were placed far from their locks."

Appendix 1 - Review of Beelzebub's Tales to His Grandson in Russian

He also used to say: "Everything is in Beelzebub, including how to make an omelette."[13]

Let us note here *en passant* that in the first and last chapters Mr. G, addressing himself to the reader, uses the formal **ВЫ** = you, while in the body of the *Tales* Beelzebub addresses his grandson (and thus, by proxy, his pupils) and is himself addressed by Hassein (no **e** as spelt in Russian) familiarly as **ТЫ** = thou, still normal between relatives and friends in Russian and in French.

Freemasonry is "A peculiar system of morality, veiled in allegory and illustrated by symbols"[14] says one of its ritual catechisms. According to the DICTIONARY, "peculiar" means "belonging exclusively to, particular, special" and the word "morality" here has its medieval significance of "education" or of "method of teaching", which was also used in the designation "Morality Plays" given to certain religious means of presenting Christian ideas (in particular about "good and evil") to illiterate people in the form of a stage play. It seems that the above definition would equally suit *Beelzebub's Tales*, with the addition that it is also, like the Judeo-Christian "Bible" and most other "Sacred Scriptures", a "coded document" which can be read in more than one way and understood on several levels.

Herein lies a trap: in its existing translations into English, in quite a number of places the words used do NOT truly and/or fully correspond to the original Russian, thus permitting, and even encouraging, rather fantastic interpretations of the sentence or passage. Thus, for example, on page 21 of the 1950 edition (page 19 of the 1992 one) the red-peppers eating Kurd is addressed as "you Jericho jackass"[15], while the Russian text says simply "**Иерихонский**" = Jericho **idiot** (so

---

[13] This was first communicated to me in 1990 by Marguerite Jure, a pupil of Mr. G; see also page 22, middle column, of TELOS, Vol. 6, No. 3, Summer 2000.

[14] *Manual Of Freemasonry* by Richard Carlile, Published by William Reeves, London, no date; p. 32.

[15] In her paper *AN Inquiring Look At The "Arousing Of Thought" Chapter* (*Applying the Hermetic Code*), Joy Lonsdale (*ALL AND EVERYTHING 2000 PROCEEDINGS*, page 91) gives the following symbolical "interpretation" based on these two mistranslations. On the word "jackass" she builds the following: "The mention of a 'Jericho jackass' has much significance, for if we remember the story of the Initiate Jesus riding upon an ass into Jerusalem, via way of Jericho, the inner meaning of Gurdjieff's little cameo should be apparent - it is the allegorical way of showing that the conscious mind is about to be carried across the barrier to the city, the subconscious. To achieve this, the initiate must Work and burn with intense effort so that his whole face (his conscious mind) is aflame (with the heat of concentration) and his eyes (allowing him to see with inner understanding) stream with the tears (or sweat) of such effort. (I wish to mention here that Nicolas has informed me that the word 'jackass' has been misstranslated from the Russian and should in fact be 'idiot'; I feel this does not alter the basic interpretation, for our Kurd 'carries on to the very end' of the process and would thus become a 'super idiot' able to enter Jerusalem, the subconscious)." And about the happening near her grave on the 40th day after his grandmother's death, Joy writes: "He states further that instead of then *standing quietly* (a requirement of his

correctly translated in the French, page 25, though unfortunately, and surprisingly, adding to the word idiot the qualification "triple" which is NOT part of the original Russian). It is not for nothing that the Italians have the saying: "Traductore tradditore"= A translator is a traitor!

Another, and utterly astonishing, not to say ridiculous, mistranslation is that of the song the infant Gurdjieff was singing while dancing around his grandmother's grave (p. 29, 1950 version): "... Now that she's turned up her toes"!?! [15] The Russian is: "**Человек она была не простои**" = She was not a simple human being, rendered somewhat oddly and incorrectly, in the 1992 English version (p. 27) as: "She was a rare one, goodness knows!" Strangely, the French version (p. 33) also translates these simple words quite incorrectly: "C'était une petite femme toute en or" (= She was a little woman wholly made of gold), thus potentially leading some would be commentators on the symbolic meaning into a false "alchemical" trail by the word "or" = gold.

Quite incomprehensibly even some quite simple and straightforward Russian words have been translated into English by words with a, sometimes quite, different meaning. Thus the name of Chapter 18, given in English as the ARCH-PREPOSTEROUS, in Russian is **АРХИФАНТАЗИЯ** = Archifantasy (that is, Utter Fantasy), so correctly translated in the French. Why these inaccuracies, I cannot imagine. Nor can I believe the so often made statement that Mr. G "approved" the English translation published in 1950. Surely, however badly Mr. G may have known English, he could read it well enough to consult a Russian-English dictionary and check whether the right word was used? Is his apparent acquiescence to a faulty translation a hint that one must never rely on another's opinion, but only on one's own experience? In this case, on reading *Beelzebub's Tales* in the original, that is, in Russian.

And now we must come to the so intriguing and important, strange, complicated and often hard to pronounce more than 400 special "Words" Mr. G uses in all his writings. Some call them "neologisms", but I prefer the more accurate, though seldom used, technical term *hapax legomena*.[2]

In both English translations they have been transliterated quite inconsistently, the same Russian letter being rendered in English in different ways. For instance, the Russian letter **X** has been transliterated sometimes as **kh** and at other times simply as **h** and once even by a **K**![16]

Some Russian letters cannot be transliterated by a single English letter (for example, the sound of the letter **Ш** has to be transliterated by **shch**), thus inducing in error those who have tried to find

---

previous meditation) he started *skipping round the grave* as if *dancing* (the inference being that he was as if 'reborn' ...). The little verse at the end reiterates the *reversal* procedure by telling us *she's turned up her toes* (reversed the thought process) and can *now with the saints repose* (begin initiate work in earnest)."

[16] In Russian in Mukransky, the 3rd letter is X, NOT k, and the Russian word MYX is the plural of FLY (the insect). Is this an additional sly hint at the importance of Beelzebub, The Lord of the Flies?

Appendix 1 - Review of Beelzebub's Tales to His Grandson in Russian

the possible roots of these words, and so, basing themselves on the English rendering, subdivide some of the word in what is the middle of a single letter in Russian!

As I understand it, Mr. G used these words partly to "bury the dog deeper"[17] and so force the reader to delve more deeply into what the word does really mean, and partly because the vibrations produced when such a word is voiced aloud[18] has a definite action on the psyche and/or the spirit, and perhaps even on the organic body, of the pupil attempting to fathom this word's true significance.

Actually, it is also surprising that occasionally one of the Russian letters has been transliterated by an English letter that does not even have the same sound as the Russian letter used by Mr. G. Thus the very first *hapax legomenon* used in the *Tales* (page 35 of the 1st and page 31 of the 2nd English versions), **Геропас**, is transliterated as Heropass inspite of the fact that its first letter, **Г**, has the sound of a hard **G** as in **God**, NOT of an **H** as in **Hero**. I suppose that the final **s** was doubled in English (but not in French), to indicate that it is pronounced and not mute.

I am, therefore, very happy to learn that in the "Second Edition" (now in preparation) of their *Guide and Index to G. I. Gurdjieff's All and Everything*, the TRADITIONAL STUDIES PRESS are going to give all these *legomena* in Cyrillic letters, side by side with the transliteration as made in the English translation. This will give the possibility to the keen and earnest worker in Mr. G's vineyard to pronounce these so special words with their right sound-vibrations.

---

[17] See Nicolas Tereshchenko's letter on the origin and meaning of this expression in Vol. 6, No. 4 Fall 2000 issue of TELOS, p. 2.

[18] Many ancient Sages and even Mr. G himself maintain that everything is created by and made up of vibrations. Even the Gospels tell us: *"In the beginning was the Word, and the Word was with God, and the Word was God... All things were made by him; and without him was not any thing made that was made."* (St; John 1:1 & 3). Let us not forget also that in all prayers and invocations originating in Hebrew it is the NAME of "God" (that is, the vibration produced by pronouncing it aloud) which is most important; thus the Qabalistic most Holy Divine Name, the Sacred Four-Letter Name known as the "Tetragrammaton" יהוה (YOD-HEY-VAV-HEY), must NEVER be pronounced aloud, except once a year by the High Priest alone in the Holy of Holies of the Temple; in fact many believe that its true pronunciation has been forgotten if not altogether lost (but initiates of some Orders, such as the Rosicrucian Order Alpha and Omega, the only legitimate heir and successor of the legendary Hermetic Order of the Golden Dawn, say that their High Grade Adepts do know this true pronunciation). Another Divine four-letter Name (Exodus 3:14) is אהיה (ALEF-HEY-YOD-HEY) and rings a Gurdjieffian bell as it means I AM, and, according to Qabalists, really expands into "I AM He who was, is and ever shall be". Note also that in the Christian "Lord's Prayer" (Luke 11:2) it is said *"Our Father... hallowed be **Thy Name**..."*, NOT *"be **Thou** hallowed"*. Finally, Our Lord Jesus Christ said (Matthew 18:20): *"For when Two or three are assembled in my Name, I AM (εἰμί in Greek) there in the midst of them."* And we all know what great importance Mr. G attached to the I AM exercise: see, for example, TELOS, Vol. 6, No. 3 Summer 2000, pp. 8, 9, 18 & 22.

But there is no need to multiply the examples where the Russian and the English texts differ. The only, according to me, logical deduction on the basis of this proven weakness of and inaccuracy in all translations is that ALL those who *really and truly* wish to study and understand *Beelzebub's Tales To His Grandson*, to find "where the dog is buried", to bring the keys and their locks together, to make their own everything Mr. G wished to transmit to us through *Beelzebub's Tales*, thus becoming authentic "Beelzebub's Grandchildren" and not only "Companions of the Book", MUST learn Russian to be able to read Mr. G's legacy as he wrote it and thus base all their symbolic and other interpretations on the true text and not on a lesser or greater deformation of it.

But we must be realists: it is unlikely that many people will have the time, the opportunity, the will-power and the ability to learn a new language, especially one as rich in words as Russian. So most of those who follow THE WORK must be content with the existing English translation(s), until a new and better one becomes available. It would be a great help, though, if the exact pronunciation of all the hapax legomena were available on disk or cassette, just as Mr. G's music is now available.

At any rate, the best way I know of concluding this review is to say: Thank you Mister Gurdjieff, Teacher of Dances, for making available to us the wisdom of this great ancient and previously unknown Teaching transmitted in your chef-d'œuvre **РАССКАЗЫ ВЕЛЬЗЕВУЛА СВОЕМУ ВНУКУ!**

Addendum: Who is Beelzebub in the Western Esoteric Tradition?

The name "Beelzebub" (**ВЕЛЬЗЕВУЛ** in Russian) is a corruption of BAAL ZEBUB (כעל וכוכ in Hebrew), which means "Lord of Flies" and thus also probably, by extension, of all insects. The spelling of this Entity's name varies quite a lot in different texts and languages, being, for example: Baalzebul, Beelzebul, Belzaboul, Belzebuth, Belzebud, Beelzebub, etc...

In the beginning, he was a Syrian God, but in the *Old Testament* (2 Kings 1:2-16) we find him as the "god of Ekron". In the *New Testament* (Matthew 10:25 & 12:24; Marc 3:22; Luke 11:15 & 18-19 who spell this name **Βεελξεβουλ** in Greek), he is already the "Prince of Demons" and this is also his title according to the "Great Grimoire" (in which Lucifer is the "Emperor" and Astaroth the "Grand Duke" of demons). In his Gnostic writings, Valentine gives him the designation of "Lord of Chaos".

In the *Testament of Solomon*, King Solomon, having received from Yahwe (יהוה) a magic ring, evokes through its power various spirits and entities. When Beelzebub is called, Solomon begins to interrogate him by the question: "Who are you?", and Beelzebub answers that he is the Chief of Demons, to whom it is he who gives the power to become visible to human eyes. On Solomon's demand, Beelzebub makes appear a female spirit, named Onoskelis, whom Solomon immediately sets to work and orders to start twisting the ropes that will later be used in the Temple whose construction he had just began.

Appendix 1 - Review of Beelzebub's Tales to His Grandson in Russian

In the *Grimorium Verum*, Beelzebub is one of the three Chiefs of Demons (the two others being, again, Lucifer and Astaroth). His two lieutenants are "Tarchimache" and "Fleurity" and his preferred place of residence is Africa. When he is evoked, he appears either in the shape of a gigantic Bull (in a state of erection) or of a Goat with a very long tail, of which he is very proud. When angry, he vomits flames.

From the apocryphal Gospel known as the *Testament of Nicodemus* (a Jewish "Elder" who, together with Joseph of Arimathea, took down from the cross the body of Our Lord and Grand Master Jesus-Christ and carried Him to the tomb), we learn (18:14 and 19:7-12) that when Jesus descended into Hell after His death on the cross, Our Lord gave Beelzebub dominion over Satan (and consequently over all demons) as a reward for having agreed to the liberation of Adam and of all the other "saints in prison", whom the Christ then took to Paradise with Him. In fact, until that day (i.e. Our Lord's death on the cross), all those who had died, including even all the "saints" and "prophets", were in "Hell" (the Jews' "Sheol" – שאול and the Greeks' "Gehenna" – Γεεννα, "Hades" - Ἅδης or "Tartaros" - Ταρταρος).

In Paradise, apart from God and His angels, there were only three other persons: Enoch and Elias (who both, after their elevation direct to Heaven without having to die, were promoted to the rank of Archangels, named, respectively, Metattron and Sandaiphon) and the "good thief" to whom Christ had promised (Luke 23:43) that to-day (the day of his death) he will be in Paradise.

© Copyright 2001 - Nicolas Tereshchenko - All Rights Reserved

Appendix 2 - List of Attendees

Harry Bennett - USA
Pat Bennett - USA
Anthony Blake - UK
Len Brown - CANADA
Nikolas Bryce - CANADA
Frank Brzeski - UK
Keith Buzzell - USA
Anne Clark - USA
Wim Van Dullemen - HOLLAND
Stefanos Elmazis - GREECE
Ana Helena Fragomeni - BRAZIL
Sy Ginsburg - USA
Susan Hagan - UK
Christiane Macketanz - GERMANY
William Y. Murphy - USA
Marlena O'Hagan-Buzzell - USA
Alison Perrott – UK
John Perrott - UK
Bonnie Phillip - USA
June Poulton - USA
John Scullion - UK
H. J. (Bert) Sharp - UK
Karen Stefano - USA
Nicolas Tereshchenko - AUSTRALIA
Chris Thompson - UK
Prof. M. W. Thring - UK
Dorothy Usiskin - USA
Sofia Wellbeloved - UK
Steven Wheeler - UK

Index

A

Abrustdonis 36, 114, 115
Absolute 35, 38
active 32, 47, 66, 81, 118, 121
Adrenaline 119
Africa 108, 155
Ahoon 46, 48, 49
Aim 26, 27, 36, 38, 44, 46, 56, 58, 60, 76, 78, 80, 131, 147
air 18, 24, 46, 74, 115, 118, 119, 139
Akhaldan 54
alcohol 64
Salzmann, de, Jean; Michel 13, 22, 23, 64, 65, 66, 144, 145, 149
allegorical 89, 151
allegory 128, 151
Amber 53, 54, 57
America 10, 63, 65, 68, 99, 106, 108, 140
Anderson, Margaret 65, 114, 121, 150
Angel . 50, 52, 55, 61, 99, 107, 110, 111, 118, 155
Anklad 38
Anulios 37, 41
Arcanum 147
Archangel 50, 55, 60, 155
Aristotle 34, 103, 117
armagnac 64, 65, 71
Armenia 21
Armenian 149, 150
ascending 18, 121
Ashish, Sri Madhava 12
Askokin 36, 37
astral 118
Astrology 136, 148
Atlantis 27, 115
Atom 63

Attention.. 17, 19, 26, 28, 55, 63, 73, 77, 113, 121
awareness 29, 38, 84, 102, 108, 109, 119, 123
axis 19, 70

B

Beelzebub.. 5, 6, 8, 10, 23, 24, 31, 34, 40, 45, 46, 47, 48, 49, 50, 54, 55, 56, 57, 60, 61, 63, 64, 65, 69, 72, 75, 76, 77, 87, 88, 102, 112, 113, 114, 115, 116, 119, 124, 125, 126, 135, 136, 137, 144, 145, 147, 148, 149, 150, 151, 152, 154, 155
Beelzebub's Tales
   The Tales 45, 49, 76, 86, 125, 137, 138, 148, 151, 153
Being . 5, 9, 15, 16, 17, 19, 27, 32, 34, 35, 36, 37, 38, 40, 42, 43, 46, 47, 48, 50, 51, 53, 54, 56, 57, 58, 60, 61, 62, 63, 69, 70, 71, 75, 81, 83, 85, 87, 88, 90, 97, 98, 99, 100, 104, 105, 106, 108, 110, 112, 113, 114, 115, 117, 118, 119, 120, 121, 123, 124, 125, 126, 127, 129, 130, 133, 134, 135, 136, 138, 145, 147, 148, 149, 152, 154, 155
being-bodies 60, 112, 113, 114, 135, 138
being-mentation 38
Belcultassi 131
Bennett, John G... 7, 8, 10, 12, 13, 32, 63, 64, 65, 68, 69, 70, 72, 88, 97, 98, 114, 156
Blake, Anthony 1, 8, 9, 87, 97, 156
Blavatsky, Helena P. 82
Bliss 67
Bogachevsky 127
bone 31
Brain 32, 35, 37, 41, 44, 75, 76, 83, 84, 85, 102, 104, 106, 107, 108, 109, 112, 119, 123, 127

157

breathe 54, 74
brother 11
Buzzell, Keith 1, 3, 6, 7, 8, 12, 75, 78, 156

C

Canada 144
carbon 63
carriage 27, 28, 42
Castanios-Flores, John 10, 12
Causal 34
center 10, 17, 19, 24, 25, 26, 27, 28, 29, 32, 41, 42, 46, 48, 49, 54, 55, 63, 85, 98, 101, 115, 119, 120, 124, 127, 138
centrifugal 59
Chakra 120
    Ajna 121
    Anahata 121
    Manipura 121
    Sahasrara 121
    Svadhisthana 121
    Visuddha 121
cherubim 34
child 48, 62, 125, 126, 136
children ... 13, 71, 72, 119, 125, 128, 130, 149
Chinese 67
Christ 23, 99, 126, 153, 155
Christian 118, 151, 153
Christianity 101
coat 60, 113
    coated 36, 38, 113
    coating 29, 36, 38, 112, 113, 114, 115
comet 48
concentrate 32, 35, 38, 60, 151
concentration 32, 35, 38, 60, 151
Conscience 14, 28, 29, 42, 44, 62, 63, 73, 128, 129, 130
conscious 26, 28, 31, 32, 34, 35, 36, 44, 75, 76, 104, 105, 106, 107, 108, 109, 110, 112, 113, 115, 119, 128, 129, 131, 151
Conscious Labor 34, 35, 36, 44, 112, 113
consciousness 25, 27, 36, 37, 48, 78, 105, 108, 109, 110, 122, 128, 131, 148
contemplate 85

contemplation 27, 85, 149
Coombe Springs 72
Cortex 107, 127
cosmic .. 14, 25, 28, 29, 35, 38, 48, 52, 57, 84, 85, 102, 112, 113, 126
cosmology 58
Creation 29, 52, 55, 58, 65, 70, 82, 84, 108, 110, 148
creative 117, 121
Creator 46
Creed, Lewis 10, 12
Cryptomnesia 105, 117
crystallize
    crystallization 112
    crystallized 38, 50, 84, 113, 122

D

daughter 11, 12, 16, 63
death 10, 12, 18, 22, 76, 82, 114, 145, 150, 151, 155
Denying 100
Dervish 76, 121, 123
Descartes, Rene 31, 32
descend 100
descending 18
descent 58
Deskaldino 45
devil 145, 150
Dicker, The 10, 12
die 40, 42, 65, 82, 108, 130, 155
digest 47
digestion 58, 76, 84, 115, 117
dimension 42, 71
dog 14, 28, 30, 37, 40, 114, 121, 153, 154
Dramatic Universe 97
dream 105, 106, 107, 148
dying 67

E

Earth 45, 48, 49, 52, 54, 59, 81, 101, 102, 104, 110, 112, 113, 131, 149
Echmiadzin 50

Eftologodiksis 115
Ego 117, 130
    egoism 45, 48, 62
Egypt 54, 148
Egyptian 19, 103
electricity 57, 58, 72
electron 57
Elekilpomagtistzen 52, 55
element 58, 87, 90, 125, 149
emanation 59, 63, 67, 113
embryo 120
emotion 26, 29, 32, 37, 41, 42, 46, 63, 81, 83, 107, 119, 120, 122, 123
emotional ... 26, 27, 28, 29, 41, 42, 44, 48, 49, 53, 55, 58, 64, 70, 81, 82, 84, 85, 86, 101, 108, 117, 119, 120, 121, 123, 127, 128, 129
Endlessness.... 34, 35, 38, 60, 61, 81, 84, 112, 121, 126, 145
England 6, 7, 14, 68, 140
enneagon 19
Enneagram 13, 17, 18, 19, 23, 24, 25, 147, 148
entropy 57
epilepsy 107, 112, 119
esoteric 13, 103, 112, 154
Essence .. 22, 25, 26, 39, 46, 48, 75, 118, 125, 128
Eternity 111
Evil 28, 151
Evolution . 44, 58, 73, 84, 104, 109, 115, 119, 120
    evolutionary 41
Evolve 101, 104
Exercise 22, 28, 73, 82, 88, 89, 121, 122, 123, 131, 148, 153
Exioehary 112, 113, 114, 115
exoteric 103

F

Faith 27, 127, 129, 136
father 33, 48, 99, 113, 125, 126, 127, 128, 149, 153

feeding 79, 108, 115
Feeling. 32, 36, 40, 42, 43, 46, 48, 54, 61, 62, 67, 68, 70, 73, 74, 76, 81, 82, 83, 84, 85, 107, 108, 109, 110, 119, 121, 122, 123, 124, 126, 137
Fire 110
first being-food 58, 113, 114
Food 57, 58, 76, 84, 115, 118, 119
force 26, 28, 32, 55, 58, 59, 85, 123, 153
Foundation 10, 12, 145
Fourth Way 10, 11, 13, 18, 56, 147
4th Way 13, 14
France 22, 23, 140, 149
Freud 105, 130
friction 102, 131
Frontal Lobes 107

G

genital 121
George, James 53, 61
Germany 23
Gilgamesh 13
Ginsburg, Seymour 1, 3, 7, 9, 11, 12, 112, 116, 132, 156
gland 119
Gnosis 141
Gnostic 154
God 27, 31, 36, 40, 43, 44, 64, 80, 83, 99, 102, 110, 115, 117, 119, 121, 153, 154, 155
Good 25, 70
Gornahoor Harharkh 57, 58
Gospel 97, 155
gravity 25, 27, 33, 38, 57, 58, 115, 138
Great Nature 32, 37
Greek 21, 53, 82, 100, 117, 149, 153, 154
Gregorian 149
Gurdjieff, G. I..... 5, 6, 8, 9, 10, 11, 12, 13, 14, 17, 18, 19, 22, 23, 24, 25, 26, 29, 31, 32, 40, 42, 44, 45, 46, 47, 50, 51, 52, 56, 57, 58, 60, 62, 63, 64, 65, 66, 67, 68, 69, 70, 71, 72, 73, 75, 76, 77, 78, 79, 80, 82, 83, 84, 85, 86, 98, 100, 102, 103, 104, 108,

112, 113, 114, 115, 116, 117, 118, 120, 121, 133, 135, 136, 137, 138, 145, 146, 147, 148, 149, 150, 151, 152, 153, 154
Mr. G.................................81, 88, 124, 153

H

Hanbledzoin 131
Hariton 50, 52, 53, 55, 60
harmonic 148, 149
Hartmann, Thomas and Olga de 6, 10, 12, 23, 145, 149, 150
Head-Brain 119, 136
heart................................120, 121, 122, 134
heaven 11, 110, 155
Heaven 97
Hebrew..153, 154
Helkdonis 37, 114, 115
Hell..61, 88, 155
Heptaparaparshinokh 38, 115, 126
Heretical...99
Hermetic...................................117, 151, 153
Heropass..34, 153
hierarchical...................................100, 108
hierarchy..100
higher being-bodies............112, 113, 114, 115
higher being-body 38
Hindu..12
Hitler..68
Holy Affirming 32
Holy Denying 32
Holy Reconciling 32, 120
Hope ...36, 44, 63, 70, 97, 100, 103, 116, 127, 129, 132, 135, 138
Horoscope 147
hydrogen 63, 120
Hypnosis
  hypnotism.......................................50, 131

I

I Am 28, 73
Idiot...151
imagination 22, 27, 148

impartial 53, 54, 56, 85, 117, 150
impressions 26, 28, 29, 85, 115, 118, 119, 133, 137
In Search of the Miraculous.....10, 63, 65, 69, 71, 119, 123, 126, 129, 148
  Fragments 33, 69, 70, 71, 72, 73, 118
India 105
Individual...6, 29, 31, 36, 37, 38, 60, 76, 101, 104, 105, 107, 108, 121, 127, 128, 135, 147
inexactitude..23
initiation...117
insight 90
Instinctive 26, 28, 36, 47, 55, 85, 119, 121
Institute 12, 23, 98, 149
Intellectual .26, 27, 28, 29, 32, 44, 48, 54, 55, 58, 63, 81, 84, 85, 106, 117, 119, 120, 122, 125, 128, 134, 136
intention 19, 24, 45, 76, 77, 78
interconnected.......................................37
intuition 27, 32, 148
Involve 47, 85, 115
Iraniranumange 112
Itoklanoz 113

J

Jericho 151
Jerusalem 117, 151
Jesus...............23, 99, 117, 126, 151, 153, 155
Jew 155
Jewish 155
Jung, Carl G. 105
Justice 127

K

Kant, Immanuel 33
Karatas 52
Keschapmartnian 112
Kesdjan 63, 114, 118, 147
Kundabuffer 113, 122, 124, 134

L

labyrinth 19
ladder 107
laugh 72
laughter 61, 67
Law 29, 33, 34, 35, 56, 85, 114, 148
lawful 23, 76
Legominism 23, 75
Life is Real 10, 28, 51, 85, 117
light 33, 47, 99, 107, 108, 130, 147
Limbic 107, 119
Littlehampton 11, 12
Love. 16, 32, 36, 37, 40, 42, 63, 83, 119, 121, 122, 129, 130
Lucifer 154, 155

M

machine 58, 115, 122, 128
MacLean, Paul D. 119
magic 18, 154
Magician 148
magnet
    magnetic 25, 90
maintenance 29, 35, 36, 37, 148
Mars 56, 105
material.. 6, 10, 31, 34, 45, 46, 55, 57, 62, 82, 88, 89, 90, 103, 104, 105, 106, 107, 117, 119, 125, 133, 134, 135, 136
matter. 31, 37, 44, 57, 99, 102, 103, 115, 122, 128, 141, 146
Mdnel-In 26
mechanical.. 31, 100, 104, 120, 122, 128, 132
mechanicality 101
meditate 103
meditation 27, 43, 65, 66, 82, 136, 152
Meetings with Remarkable Men 5, 51, 62, 82, 124, 126, 127, 137, 149
Megalocosmos 15, 33, 35, 38, 115
mentation ... 32, 75, 76, 77, 78, 81, 82, 83, 85, 106, 107, 108, 119
mesoteric 31
Mexico 11, 12

Microcosmos 38
Milk 98
mind .. 44, 48, 51, 54, 56, 71, 81, 89, 90, 101, 102, 105, 106, 107, 108, 109, 110, 117, 119, 122, 123, 124, 136, 140, 147, 151
Mohammed 107
monastery 21, 50, 56
monk 12, 52, 56
Moon 37, 60, 65
Moore, James 10, 22, 67
Moral 31, 34
    Morality 151
Moscow 149
Moses 107, 137
mother 11, 34, 43, 61, 98, 118, 149
Mouravieff, Boris 13
Movements 6, 8, 9, 10, 12, 123
Moving 26, 28, 32, 46, 55, 63, 65, 71, 85, 108, 121, 123
Mozart 69, 123
Mullah Nassr Eddin 45
music 6, 13, 22, 23, 41, 71, 117, 120, 122, 124, 133, 136, 154
myth 55

N

Nature 3, 26, 27, 31, 32, 33, 34, 43, 52, 55, 78, 87, 88, 113, 120, 126, 132, 147
Negative emotion 41, 63
Neologism 152
nerve 107, 121, 127
neutron 58
New Age 10
Nicoll, Maurice 104
nine 18, 19, 21, 24, 85, 130, 147
ninth 147
nothing 13, 33, 34, 37, 38, 39, 42, 53, 82, 97, 98, 101, 102, 104, 119, 125, 131, 135, 138, 148, 152
Nothingness 35
Nyland, W 10, 122

O

Objective 15, 19, 25, 26, 27, 28, 29, 38, 39, 48, 50, 52, 54, 63, 85, 147, 148
Obligolnian 13, 36
octave 18, 22, 25, 46, 84, 119, 120
Okidanokh..38, 52, 53
Oldham, Ronald and Muriel 10, 12
Omnipresent...38, 52
one-brained 113, 127
ontology 5, 8, 31, 32, 33, 37, 40
Orage, Alfred 10, 11, 113, 114, 119
organic...........36, 73, 104, 107, 112, 117, 153
organon 117
Oskiano 5, 6, 9, 27, 48, 124, 125, 127, 130, 135, 137
Ouspensky, P. D...5, 6, 13, 14, 33, 40, 41, 62, 63, 64, 67, 68, 69, 70, 71, 72, 73, 119, 127, 136

P

Parable..46, 125
paradise 61, 67, 126, 155
Paris....5, 8, 11, 13, 14, 17, 19, 22, 23, 24, 62, 63, 64, 66, 69, 73, 134, 145, 150
Partkdolg-duty................32, 38, 112, 113, 135
patience 82
personality..22, 25, 26, 28, 29, 43, 48, 55, 80, 84, 105, 118, 121, 122, 131
Philadelphia...12
photon 33
physical 33, 40, 41, 43, 44, 58, 70, 81, 83, 84, 85, 109, 113, 119, 120, 121, 123, 125, 126, 128, 136
physics..31, 33
Planck, Max 33
planet..38, 45, 46, 48, 52, 56, 60, 84, 99, 101, 102, 112, 113, 115, 122, 138
planetary 46, 63, 102, 147
Podkoolad 38
Pogossian 50, 128
politics 99
ponder 35, 43, 61, 135

pondering 29, 43
Popoff, Irmis 12, 137
Pray 121
Prayer 21, 27, 153
presence 29, 32, 35, 36, 37, 38, 105, 107, 110
Priest 153
Prieure......................................10, 11, 22, 23, 72
Prime Source 38
Protein...84
Protocosmos..35, 38
proton..58
psyche 37, 85, 153
psychological 10, 12, 45, 50, 51, 74, 104, 128, 138
psychology..26, 28, 98, 148
Psychology of Man's Possible Evolution ...71
Ptolemy...100
Purgatory.27, 59, 60, 61, 69, 84, 85, 113, 114
Pythagoras...22
Pythagorean 18

Q

Qabalistic 153
Qabalists 153
Quantum 56
quintessence 13

R

Ray of Creation.....................................18, 22
Reason..15, 27, 29, 33, 38, 39, 48, 61, 63, 69, 70, 99, 114, 120, 125, 128, 129, 138, 142, 147
Reciprocal..37
Reconcile
  Reconciliation 29
redemption 55
religion 10, 21, 42, 71, 102
Remember 60, 66, 67, 70, 71, 73, 82, 87, 102, 140, 142, 151
  Remembering...73
Reptilian 119
resonance 83, 84, 86, 124, 128

Index

resonate 86, 124
Rosicrucian 153
Rumi, Jalaluddin 16
Russia 5, 51, 64, 67, 70, 77, 102, 136, 137, 144, 145, 147, 148, 149, 150, 151, 152, 153, 154

S

Sacred 6, 8, 13, 21, 22, 23, 29, 35, 36, 38, 42, 43, 64, 112, 114, 151, 153
sacrifice 16, 81, 82
Salle Pleyel 5, 17, 22, 23, 24, 66
Sarmoung (also Surmang)
  Sarmoun 50
Satan 155
Saturn 57
Schrödinger 35, 55, 57
Science 10, 12, 13, 31, 33, 34, 37, 40, 41, 42, 43, 44, 54, 97, 104, 117, 148, 149, 150
Scientific 34, 37, 42, 44, 78, 147
seeing 41, 68, 81, 84, 87, 88, 97, 102, 128, 130, 131
Self 25, 73, 84, 109, 131, 148
Self Observation 122, 130, 131
Self Remembering 73
Self-consciousness 27, 48
sensation 29, 74, 75, 76, 81, 86, 122, 124
senses 28, 32, 34, 40, 44
Sensing 63, 66, 82
Sensory 32, 43, 109, 124
seraphim 34
serpent 55
seven 18, 21, 25, 88, 89, 149
Sex 25, 40
  sexual 112, 119
Shah, Idries 87
Sharp, H. J. (Bert) 1, 8, 41
shock 19
Shushumna 121
sing 122
singing 152
sister 68, 69

Sitting 8, 9, 42, 44, 47, 63, 64, 65, 99, 134, 135
Sleep 25, 106
Sly Man 148
Smith, Russell A. 13, 25
snake 29
solar plexus 32
son 85
Sophia 8, 45, 50, 148
Soul 31, 63, 101, 114, 118, 147
sound 88, 145, 149, 152, 153
spinal column 32
Spirit 16, 46, 72, 97, 149, 153, 154
  spiritual 34, 40, 42, 43, 57, 72, 98, 99, 100, 101, 118, 147, 148
St. Petersburg (also Petersburg) 149
Stalin 68
Staveley, A.L. 12
Stopinder 38, 141
subconscious 76, 148, 151
subconsciousness 128
subjective 36, 37, 75, 76, 80, 85, 120
substance . 31, 37, 41, 52, 112, 113, 118, 122, 132
Subud 13
Suffer
  Intentional Suffering ... 34, 35, 36, 44, 112, 113
  suffered 64, 67, 149
  suffering 104, 129
Sun 19, 34, 35, 38, 59, 60, 83, 147
Sun Absolute 34, 35, 38
Symbol 17, 53, 54, 63
  symbolic . 41, 45, 51, 56, 57, 110, 152, 154
  symbology 13, 52
Synchronicity 123

T

Tail 62, 155
Tarot 147
Tereshchenko, Nicolas 1, 9, 11, 12, 13, 77, 112, 116, 153, 155, 156
Tetartocosmos 38, 84, 112

Tetragrammaton 153
The Fourth Way 148
Theomertmalogos 84, 145
Theosophical 12
Third Force 120
Thompson, Chris 24, 156
three-brained 29, 32, 34, 35, 36, 38, 39, 61, 76, 77, 84, 85, 104, 112, 113, 114, 120, 136
   3 brained 125, 126, 127
Thring, M.W., Prof.1, 6, 8, 14, 24, 31, 39, 40, 41, 42, 43, 44, 52, 56, 62, 67, 69, 71, 72, 73, 74, 121, 156
time ..6, 13, 14, 22, 23, 26, 27, 28, 31, 32, 34, 35, 36, 37, 38, 40, 42, 45, 46, 47, 50, 52, 54, 55, 56, 57, 58, 59, 61, 63, 64, 66, 67, 68, 70, 71, 75, 81, 82, 84, 85, 86, 88, 89, 90, 97, 98, 101, 102, 103, 104, 105, 106, 107, 109, 110, 112, 113, 114, 115, 117, 118, 119, 120, 121, 123, 125, 126, 128, 130, 133, 135, 137, 138, 139, 140, 143, 145, 147, 154
Toomer, Jean 11
transform 36, 47
transformation ..5, 10, 12, 17, 25, 26, 57, 118, 125
transmute 36
Triad 25, 76, 127
Triangle Editions 144, 145
Trinity 21, 63
Tritocosmos 38
Trogoautoegocrat 35
two-brained 32, 81, 113

U

unconscious 101, 105, 106, 107, 117
understanding 5, 31, 32, 33, 34, 35, 40, 43, 54, 79, 99, 107, 108, 112, 119, 120, 122, 126, 127, 131, 147, 148, 151

universe 35, 36, 37, 40, 55, 57, 58, 63, 70, 83, 100, 101, 113, 115, 148, 149
USA 7, 22, 28, 30, 156

V

Venoma 50, 51, 55, 60, 61
vibration.24, 37, 38, 40, 41, 42, 44, 113, 121, 123, 146, 153
visudda 121
vivifyingness 38

W

Washington 11, 142
Water 46, 82, 88, 118
Webb, James 23
Wellbeloved, Sophia 8, 45, 156
Wisdom 101, 105, 106, 127, 154
Word 153
Work 10, 12, 13, 24, 28, 63, 67, 69, 76, 82, 125, 126, 128, 129, 130, 148, 149, 151
world 16, 29, 31, 34, 36, 41, 43, 52, 57, 62, 63, 65, 76, 77, 79, 80, 82, 83, 84, 85, 86, 98, 99, 101, 102, 110, 112, 114, 123, 137, 141, 145, 149

Y

Yelov 50
Yoga 103, 120, 148
   Haida 148
   Kundalini 120
   Tantric 103

Z

Zilnotrago 45, 46, 47
Zodiac 148

The Proceedings of the 6th International Humanities Conference: All & Everything 2001

The All & Everything Conference has become established as an independent forum on the Work of G. I. Gurdjieff, attracting international scholars, artists, scientists, group leaders, students, and speakers from around the world.

The All & Everything Conference provides an open, congenial and serious atmosphere for the sharing of researches and investigations of Gurdjieff's legacy. The Conference seeks to keep the study of the teachings of Gurdjieff relevant to global scientific, spiritual and sociological developments. The Conference includes the presentation of academic papers, individual view papers, seminars on the chapters and themes in All & Everything, and relevant cultural events.

The All and Everything Conferences are totally non-sectarian, and not presented under the auspices or sponsorship of any Gurdjieff Group or umbrella organization. The Conferences are and will remain entirely independent. They are organized by a volunteer Planning Committee of students from many countries, supported by a diverse volunteer Advisory Board and Reading Panel composed of academics and prominent students of Gurdjieff's teaching.

www.aandeconference.org

This Copy has been Printed from the Proceedings eBook:

ISBN 9781905578214

Gurdjieff / Fourth Way / Western Esotericism / Spirituality

www.ingramcontent.com/pod-product-compliance
Lightning Source LLC
Chambersburg PA
CBHW080921180426
43192CB00040B/2605